BADGER ASSEMBLY STORIES

WITH CITIZENSHIP AND PSHE THEMES

Ages 7-11

Andy and Barbara Seed

Badger Publishing

26 Wedgwood Way, Pin Green Industrial Estate, Stevenage, Hertfordshire SG1 4QF
Telephone: 01438 356907 Fax: 01438 747015

Cover photograph: Educational Solutions Ltd

INTRODUCTION

This book contains 32 assemblies for children aged 7-11, written specifically to resource the Non-statutory guidelines for PSHE and Citizenship at Key Stage 2. Each assembly begins with an introduction and then a main presentation, usually given by the teacher. There are both interactive and non-interactive follow-up ideas and every assembly concludes with an optional reflection or prayer. The assemblies use a wide range of stimulus material:

- Original stories
- Fiction: excerpts from children's books
- 'True life' stories: factual accounts of people's lives
- Factual accounts of events
- Information, e.g. how a book is made
- Mini drama sketches for children to perform, with play scripts
- Poems

Each assembly focuses on a single teaching requirement from the four strands of the PSHE and Citizenship guidelines, as listed in the contents and on the relevant assembly pages.

Follow up

Each assembly presentation is followed by suggestions for interaction to involve the audience in the assembly, and to reinforce learning. Interactive follow up activities include:

- Closed and open questions
- Active response, e.g. vote, hands up, thumbs up or down, giving scores
- Quizzes
- Use of volunteers to assist at the front
- Discussion

Non-interactive follow up suggestions include:

- A summary of the story
- Points to think about
- Reflection and prayer

Using the material

The assemblies in the book are designed to be used flexibly: it is intended that teachers select the most appropriate follow up activities and questions from the range provided in order to meet the needs of the children present. The basic core presentation of each assembly may also be adapted to suit the school, of course, and may be used, for example, in circle time, as the basis for role-play or other drama or for classroom discussion in Citizenship lessons. Questions to stimulate response from the children might include:

- What might it feel like to be in this situation?
- Have you experienced a situation like this in real life?
- Why did the characters do what they did?
- Were they right/wrong?

What makes a successful assembly?

Good preparation is essential, particularly if drama is involved. Other key pointers:

- Use of props or a visual focus (suggestions are included in the book; don't forget an OHP or data projector can be used if you can't find the object suggested).
- Relate the contents of the assembly to activities going on in the school or community.
- Interactivity: music, songs, drama or any kind of audience participation generates interest.
- Use the story or presentation to make a single clear learning point, which can be reinforced in the reflection or prayer at the end of the assembly.

CONTENTS

1A GIVING YOUR OPINION

Objective
To help children to think about topical issues and give their opinions.

PSHE/Citizenship links
1a (Opinions)

Props
(Not essential): a light bulb

Introduction
The light bulb is a great invention. It helps our lives so much. Just think what it would be like if we still had to use candles all the time, or smelly oil lamps which needed to be filled and cleaned endlessly. But light bulbs don't work by themselves – they need electricity, of course. And electricity doesn't just happen – it has to be made. But where's the best place to make it I wonder, and how?

STORY: NOT IN MY BACK YARD!

"Mrs Benson! Have you heard about the wind farm?" Selina was still out of breath. She'd run across the village green to be the first into school so that she could tell her teacher the news.

"You look a bit excitable today Selina – and you're very early – it's only half past eight you know."

"I know, I'm sorry Mrs Benson, but my next door neighbour Mr Billingham said that there's going to be a big wind farm built up on the moor behind the village."

"Well, actually, Selina, I do know quite a lot about it – in fact I've planned for the class to have a little talk about it today after assembly."

Selina went out into the tiny playground at the front of her school. The school was situated in a small village high up in the Yorkshire Dales, and the view across the hills was spectacular. It also meant that she could see everyone approaching from the road below, and soon there was a gaggle of juniors standing by the wall sheltering from the wind. Everyone was talking about the wind farm.

"But what is a wind farm?" said Robert.

"It's a whole load of wind turbines – giant ones – that make electricity," said Selina.

"Oh, like huge windmills you mean?"

"That's right."

"But why are they building one up here?"

"My mum says it's because it's very windy and no one lives up there on the moors." This conversation continued for some time until the bell rang and the children trudged indoors.

After assembly, Mrs Benson began to tell Selina's class a bit more about the wind farm. "You've probably heard the news that there may be something called a wind farm built on Bracken Moor up behind the village," said Mrs Benson. "Well, nothing has been decided for sure, but the moor has been chosen as the best location for a wind farm by the electricity company. But they can't just go ahead and build it until everyone has had their say at a big meeting called a planning inquiry.

"Right, well let's just make sure everyone knows what a wind farm is first. Who can explain?" Selina's friend Mel put up her hand and Mrs Benson nodded for her to speak.

"It's a big collection of tall wind turbines which make electricity."

"That's right – very good Melanie. And who can explain how a wind turbine works?"

"Oh, I know," said Tom Calvert, waving his hand excitedly.

"Go on then Tom," said Mrs Benson.

"Right, a wind turbine is just the same as a windmill – it's a tall tower with propeller blades. The wind turns them and that moves machinery inside to make electricity – each one has a generator. The electricity goes along cables from the turbines to homes and factories."

"Excellent, Tom," said the teacher. "Does anyone know any more about them?"

A few more hands went up and Mrs Benson made a list of facts on the board:

- 30 turbines proposed to be built.
- Each one 60 metres tall.
- Make enough electricity for 20,000 homes.
- Blades turn slowly.

"Now, my next question is, why does the electricity company want to build this wind farm when there are already lots of power stations in other places making electricity?"

This time Selina answered the question. "We were talking about it at home, and my dad says we need more ways to make power because people use more and more electricity nowadays – we all have loads of computers and TVs and things that have to be plugged in."

"That's true," said Mrs Benson. "But why don't they just build another coal-burning power station in a coal-mining area?"

"Coal is running out," said Robert. "And burning coal makes loads of pollution."

More hands went up.

"And wind turbines don't make air pollution, like smoke, because they don't burn anything," said Tom.

"The wind is free too, but it costs a lot to dig coal deep out of the ground," added Mrs Benson. "So it seems that the wind farm is a very good idea – it makes clean, green electricity and the wind will never run out. So why are a lot of people in the village very angry about the wind farm?"

This time, nearly every person in Selina's class put up a hand. It seemed that everyone had been talking about it at home. Mrs Benson quickly pointed at each person and made a note of the answers. All sorts of interesting things were said:

"Wind turbines are very expensive to make."

"Sometimes it's too windy up on the moors, and sometimes there's hardly any wind."

"They're really noisy – you can hear them from a kilometre away."

"They'll spoil the wild look of the moors."

"Animal habitats will be destroyed."

6

"They're massive and they look really ugly."

"People won't be allowed to walk on the moors any longer."

When everyone had been given an opportunity to speak, Mrs Benson told the class to jot down the list of reasons for and against the wind farm and to underline the three which they thought were the most important.

"What's really important though, is that everyone in the village gets a chance to say what they think about the wind farm – to give their opinion. If we don't speak up, then other people will just come along and do what they like."

After this, Mrs Benson asked everyone in the class to vote, either for or against the wind farm. 8 children voted for the wind farm and 21 voted against it.

"Why do you think more people are against the wind farm?" asked Mrs Benson. Selina answered the question.

"It's difficult, because I don't like pollution and I think wind farms are a good idea really, but building one up on the moor here will spoil the area – it's a really beautiful place."

"I think the noise would really get on our nerves," said Tom. "Our farm is right on the edge of the moor and it would scare the sheep and wreck the peace of the place."

"Thank you," said Mrs Benson. "Now, last word from the eight who voted for the wind farm – why would you choose to build it?"

Selina's friend Gill answered this time.

"Coal and oil are going to run out one day so we need to plan ahead. We need to build wind farms somewhere so why not here – there aren't many people, and you won't be able to see the turbines from down here in the valley. I agree with my big sister – she says that most people round here are nimbys who don't care that we're polluting our planet."

Mrs Benson explained that nimby stands for not in my back yard – and means people who always want things to be built somewhere else away from their homes. She then looked at the clock.

"My goodness – it's nearly quarter past ten – we should have started maths. But well done everybody – it's been a really interesting discussion." A few minutes later, everyone was filling in a worksheet about fractions. But a lot of the class were not concentrating 100% on maths – they were thinking about giant wind turbines up on the windswept moor.

I wonder if they ever did build that wind farm?

INTERACTIVE FOLLOW UP ACTIVITIES

Questions

1) Why were the class so interested in talking about the wind farm?
   (Because it might be built near to their village and would affect them.)

2) Why were most children against the wind farm?
   (Because of noise pollution, spoiling the countryside.)

3) Why did some people support the wind farm?
   (It makes electricity without pollution; fossil fuels are running out.)

7

Getting the message

1) Why is it important to have a say about issues like the wind farm?

2) The children in Mrs Benson's class gave their opinions through having a discussion. Here are some other ways to make your views known. Give them a score of 1, 5, or 10 with your fingers: 10 for the most important and useful, 1 for the least important or useful.

- Writing to a newspaper
- Going to a meeting to talk about an issue
- Demonstrating by going on a march
- Writing to you local MP or the prime minister
- Emailing a website
- Talking about it at home

Learning more

1) What is voting for?

2) What happens if people don't bother to give their opinions?

NON-INTERACTIVE FOLLOW UP

Summary of the story

- Mrs Benson's class discussed the wind farm which might be built near their village.
- They learnt that a wind farm is made up of very large turbines which make electricity.
- The class talked about the arguments for and against the wind farm.
- They found out that wind power does not cause pollution, but that it can be noisy.
- Wind farms can be expensive and can spoil the countryside for both people and wildlife.
- The class had their say and then voted.
- Mrs Benson told the class how important it was for everyone to give their opinion, or other people would decide things, possibly for the worse.

Something to think about

1) How can you give an opinion apart from speaking?

2) Why is voting important?

Reflection

The wind farm story is a good example of people having their say and helping to decide what happens in the world. It is important for you to think about issues and to come up with your own views so that you can help decide the way that things are run in the future. Try to join in discussions whenever you can.

Prayer

Lord God, thank you that we can join in discussions and share our opinions. Help us to think about important issues and also help us to listen to other people when they give their views. Help us, through talking and listening carefully, to make our world a better place. Amen.

1B SETTING GOALS

Objective
To enable children to appreciate the value of setting personal goals.

PSHE/Citizenship links
1b (Recognising their worth as individuals)

Props
(Not essential): a guitar

Introduction
Lots of people have dreams about becoming a professional sports player or famous singer or someone who travels the world. The few people who do manage to achieve their dreams usually have lots of natural talent, but there are also people who achieve dreams by setting themselves a goal and simply working hard.

STORY: STAGE WON

"Ali, you just can't sing in tune." Ali had been told this every time that he'd asked to join the school choir. He really wanted to join that choir. They all wore white shirts and stood on the stage when there was a concert and sang lovely songs. And the parents clapped them for so long. But Ali was never allowed on the stage – he would spoil it for the others.

It was the same with musical instruments. Ali was always getting told off by his teacher for tapping the drums or fiddling with the triangles during lessons. He just wanted to have a go with them. The trouble was that when he did get the chance to play them he always seemed to come in at the wrong time or play too loud.

He tried recorders once. Well, twice – he went for two lessons with the beginners' group but he just couldn't get the hang of the instrument – his fingers wouldn't stay on the holes and his blowing, well, even the teacher pulled a face of pain.

Ali begged his parents for lessons. "Can I learn the trumpet, dad? It's so cool – I saw some jazz musicians at school yesterday. Can I please? Please?"

But the answer was always the same. "We can't afford it Ali – I'm sorry."

His friends were learning instruments – the violin, the flute, the drums. It wasn't fair. Once or twice, Ali went round to a friend's house and had a go at playing an instrument, but he could never seem to get a good sound. "Maybe I'm just no good at music," he said to his mum.

"Or maybe you're just a late developer, Ali. Don't give up."

Ali had almost given up the idea of playing an instrument when he saw a girl in the street one afternoon while he was on his way to the swimming baths. She was a busker. She was standing outside the fountain singing, and making the most beautiful sound Ali had ever heard. There was a hat on the ground in front of her, and a small group of people listening intently. Ali went closer. There were lots of coins in the hat and even a couple of five pound notes. He looked at the girl. She was playing a guitar.

"That's what I'm going to do," said Ali.

The following year, Ali left primary school and went on to the Secondary School across town. It was a big change. There were thousands of kids there, so noisy and huge. And there was so much homework! Ali had to work hard almost every evening. In between essays and worksheets, he dreamt of playing the guitar. "I'll do it one day," he thought. Ali was growing up too. Before he knew it, he was in Year Eight and he was no longer one of the smallest kids in the school. He made new friends and started to get interested in football and girls. In Year Nine everyone seemed to be into clothes. Ali had never been interested in clothes and he certainly didn't have any money to spend anyway.

"You need to get yourself a Saturday job like the rest of us," said one of his friends. "Then you can get some dosh and buy some decent clothes, man."

Ali asked his uncle, who owned a fruit and vegetable shop, if he had a job going.

"I can't give you a job at the moment Ali, but go and try the hardware store on Priory Street – they might just be interested in you."

They were. Ali couldn't believe it. He just went into the shop and asked about a job and the woman said "Ok, we'll give you a try – be here at 8 o'clock on Saturday." Just like that – cool! A week later, Ali had £25 in his pocket – he couldn't believe it. The work was hard – he had to check the stock, fill the shelves and help at the tills but earning money was great. Ali spent some of his wages on clothes but he wanted to open a bank account too, and save up for something really good like a TV or a computer.

The weeks passed, the months passed, and the years too. Ali grew tall and his voice became deep. Exams were just around the corner – GCSEs. He was still working at the hardware shop though, and earning more now. He knew how to do everything that needed doing for the business and the owners were really pleased with him. He'd bought himself a TV too, although he didn't watch it much.

Ali did well in his exams and went into the sixth form at the Secondary School. This was great – no more uniform and there was the common room to hang about in. It had a microwave, fridge and loads of comfy chairs to laze about on between lessons. But the best thing was the stereo – there was a fantastic CD system there, which the students had bought themselves. Ali spent hours just listening to music with his friends and talking about their favourite tracks.

Some of his mates also talked about forming a band.

"Can you play anything Ali?" they asked.

"No way – and I sing worse than an old cat."

So Ali wasn't in the band that his friends formed, but he listened to them practise. They weren't very good, but they did have fun. Ali wished he could play something, and he thought back ruefully to the days when he really wanted to play the guitar. Hadn't he said he would do it? Yeah, but he was young then and, well, he was just no good.

But Ali kept thinking about the band and about playing the guitar. He walked past the music shop in town one day on his way home. There were three electric guitars in the window. The cheapest was £260, but it came with a small amplifier. He went into the shop.

A week later Ali was standing in his bedroom holding a brand new guitar. He flicked at the strings and imagined playing it properly. It made a great sound. Ali's friends gave him some books about learning to play and he found some simple music on the internet. At first he was really slow, and his fingers just wouldn't seem to do what they were supposed to – they got quite sore too. But it was fun, and Ali was determined to give this a real go: he had spent loads of his own hard-earned money after all.

10

After three weeks, where Ali had practised every single night, he began to get the hang of the little exercises in the book and to play a few simple tunes. He was still slow and clumsy but he was making progress. On Sundays, Ali's friends came round and gave him some tips. They laughed at him a little, but Ali knew it was only what he would have done.

"Keep going Ali, my son – you'll make the band eventually!"

And keep going he did. Without a single lesson, Ali learnt how to play the guitar. He used books, tapes, videos, and the internet, but the most important thing was his own determination to succeed. After six months he was bringing his guitar to the school with the others and joining in with band practices. Nobody actually said that they needed another guitarist, but Ali just sort of joined – he became part of the band.

And he became good: he practised and practised and practised. He learnt famous songs and played them; he stunned the teachers who had no idea that he could play anything, and even his parents recognised that he had done something remarkable.

At the end of the year, Ali's parents were among the audience at the Secondary School Celebration Evening. This was the night for certificates and awards for all the students who had done well. It was also an event where the students provided the entertainment and Ali's band were on first. As he stood on the stage with his guitar and counted in the first song, he was as amazed as everyone else.

INTERACTIVE FOLLOW UP ACTIVITIES

Questions

1) What helped Ali succeed?

   (Determination, hard work and sticking to the goal he had set himself.)

2) Who gave Ali most help?

   (He really just helped himself, although his friends did help him too.)

3) How did Ali get the guitar?

   (He bought it himself after saving his wages.)

Getting the message

1) What can we learn from this assembly?

   (Not to give up; to persevere; to set goals; don't believe that you just can't do something.)

2) Put your hand up for the true statements about the story.

   • Ali was a late developer. *(T)*

   • No one encouraged Ali. *(F)*

   • Ali was naturally gifted in music. *(F)*

   • Ali learnt the guitar through hard work and practice. *(T)*

   • Ali joined the band because he wanted to be famous. *(F)*

   • Ali reached his goal. *(T)*

Learning more

1) What other kinds of goals can people set themselves?

2) What else was Ali good at, apart from playing the guitar?

NON-INTERACTIVE FOLLOW UP

Summary of the story

- When he was young, Ali wanted to sing or play an instrument.
- Ali found music very difficult at first.
- Ali decided that one day he would learn the guitar.
- Ali went to secondary school, grew older, got a Saturday job and forgot about his goal.
- In the sixth form, Ali's friends formed a band.
- Ali bought a guitar and gradually taught himself to play.
- Ali joined the band and gave a performance on the stage at his school.

Something to think about

1) Why do some people set themselves goals?
2) What was it that helped Ali to achieve his goal?
3) Why was the story called 'Stage Won'?

Reflection

You can learn a lot from the story of Ali and his guitar. Ali succeeded in reaching his goal of playing the guitar through hard work, determination and practice. It isn't easy to teach yourself something, but it's amazing what you can do if you really try. So decide what you really want to go for and do your best.

Prayer

Lord God, thank you that you have given us all the ability to learn. Help us to reach the goals we set and help us to persevere when we feel like giving up. Give us the determination to achieve something good in our lives. Amen.

1c FACING CHALLENGES

Objective
To inspire children to meet the challenges they face.

PSHE/Citizenship links
1c (Facing challenges)

Props
(Not essential): a book

Introduction
As you're sitting here right now, you're probably not thinking, 'aren't I lucky to be at school'. Well today's story is about a boy who was desperate to go to school. He was desperate to get his hands on a book (hold up the book), and desperate to learn.

TRUE STORY: BOOKER'S BOOK

We all have challenges to face in life: growing up, making friends, moving on to secondary school, doing exams and finding a job. But if you were born a black slave, 150 years ago in America, you had to face enormous challenges. One person who did this was Booker T. Washington.

His mother was the slave of a white farmer in Virginia; Booker didn't know who his father was, but he did have a stepfather.

Booker's first challenge came when he was younger than you: he became a water boy, carrying water to the other slaves working in the fields in the baking sun. This was a hard task and there was no pay.

Then, when Booker was nine, the laws in America changed and all the slaves were set free. Booker's stepfather took the family to live in another area and Booker was forced to work in a salt mine, packing barrels. A year later, he faced another challenge when he had to work down a coal mine.

The family were extremely poor – they had little food and wore ragged clothes, but Booker knew there was one way for him to get a better job and improve himself: education. Booker's next challenge was to learn to read. At first there were no schools for black children in the USA, so Booker begged his mother to get him a book. In time, he was given a spelling book, but no one around him could read or write and so Booker had to somehow teach himself the letters.

When a school did eventually open, Booker was desperate to go but his stepfather didn't want to lose the wages that Booker's job brought in. So Booker had to go to classes at night, after he had been working all day, to learn to read and write.

When Booker was sixteen, he faced yet another tough challenge. He wanted to go to High School but was told he would have to pay for his own lessons. Amazingly, he did this by becoming the school caretaker, sweeping out the very classrooms where his lessons took place.

Booker did well at school – his teachers were impressed by his ability and also by his hard work and eagerness to learn. Eventually, the headteacher of the school arranged for Booker's fees to be paid for by a wealthy white man. When Booker left Hampton Agricultural Institute, he was grown up, but as an adult he faced his next great challenge: finding a good job.

This was very difficult in America in those days, as the country was controlled by white people who took all of the best jobs. Many of these people didn't think that blacks like Booker should be free to have the same chances as whites. But Booker had impressed everyone at his school and the college helped him to find work as a teacher at another local school.

Once again, Booker proved to be a success and after a few years he was asked to become headteacher of a new school for black children at Tuskegee. This was a wonderful opportunity for Booker, but when he saw the buildings that he was supposed to use, his heart sank – there were just a couple of tumble down shacks. So Booker had to face perhaps his greatest challenge, but like every other one he had faced, he rose to meet it with courage, determination and hard work.

With the help of his small group of students, Booker put up new buildings and built an entirely new school. He borrowed money to buy land, and by 1888, the school owned 540 acres of grounds and had 400 students. The school had become a great success, and people began to talk about Booker. Later on, he even went to give advice to the President of the USA. Once again, Booker, the man who was once a penniless slave, had met the challenge.

INTERACTIVE FOLLOW UP ACTIVITIES

Questions

1) Why was becoming headteacher of a school such a great achievement for Booker?
   (He started out as a slave; he had to overcome so many difficulties; there were few good jobs, especially important ones, for black people.)

2) What enabled him to meet all the challenges he faced?
   (Hard work, determination, ambition, courage and a desire to learn.)

3) Why was the book so important to Booker?
   (It got him started; it enabled him to begin to learn to read.)

Getting the message

1) What can we learn from this true story?
   (We can all meet challenges, even big ones, if we work hard, try our best and don't give up.)

2) Show whether these statements about Booker are true or false by giving them a thumbs-up or thumbs-down:
   - Booker had to work hard as a young child. *(T)*
   - Slaves were paid for their work. *(F)*
   - Some white people helped Booker. *(T)*
   - Many black people had good jobs in the 1800s in America. *(F)*
   - Booker found facing challenges easy. *(F)*

Learning more

1) Name some of the challenges you have had to face in life.
2) How can working hard at school help you to meet challenges?

Non-interactive Follow Up

Summary of the story

- Booker T. Washington was a poor black slave, born in the USA in the 1850s.
- He had to work as a child in the fields and in mines.
- Booker's great dream was to go to school and to learn to read and write.
- Booker went to night classes, then to a secondary school where he paid for lessons by becoming the caretaker.
- Booker worked hard and did very well at school – when he left he became a teacher.
- As a headteacher, Booker built a new school for black children, which became large and successful.

Something to think about

1) Do you have plans and dreams?
2) Do you work hard at school to give yourself the best chance of a good job later in life?
3) Do you value your teachers and other people who help you learn?

Reflection

Learn from Booker T. Washington – a poor slave boy who was determined to learn and to make himself a better person and who went on to give advice to the President of the United States. Work hard, keep trying, don't give up and do your best.

Prayer

Lord God, help us to face the challenges we meet in life. Help us to work hard, to learn, and to not give up when things are hard. Help us to overcome difficulties, like Booker T. Washington did. Amen.

1d Changing Emotions

Objective
To help children understand how emotions change at puberty.

PSHE/Citizenship links
1d (Changing emotions at puberty), 3c (Body changes at puberty)

Preparation
This assembly is in the form of a short play script or sketch, and requires four volunteer children to read a part. The ideal actors would be four good readers from Y5 or Y6 with strong clear voices – any mixture of boys and girls. A short practice before the assembly would be very helpful, and each child will need a copy of the script.

Introduction
Everyone grows up. Our bodies are programmed to get bigger as we get older until we become adults. Year sixes are bigger than Year threes and secondary school students are bigger still, on average. One day you'll become something called a teenager... but what will it be like? Here are four children to explain.

Play: Big Sisters and Brothers

A I've got an older sister.

B I've got an older brother.

C My brother's 13.

D My sister's 14.

A What's your brother like then?

B Well, until last year he was alright.

C What's he like now then?

D I've seen him – he's grown really tall.

A Just like my big sister then.

B Yeah, and he's always in a bad mood.

C Hey – so's my brother.

D My sister won't let me in her room any more.

A Mine's always on the phone: yackety yack!

B My brother's into really loud music too – the whole house shakes.

C So is mine – he never plays football with me, like he used to.

D My sister spends ages doing her greasy hair.

A Mine does that, and she's put on a lot of weight over the last year.

B Don't say that to her though – they go mad.

C They certainly do...

D My sister's got loads of spots now too.

A Why does all this happen when you grow up?

B Yeah, I don't want a deep growly voice like my brother's.

C My brother blames me for everything.

D My sister says I'm always in the way.

A So, why does all this happen?

B Yeah, *we're* not like that are we?

C My dad says it's all to do with hormones.

D Hormones? What are they?

A They're powerful chemicals which your body makes.

B That's right – my mum says that teenagers are full of hormones.

C We've all this to look forward to...

D Is that what puberty is then?

A Yes, it's when your body changes loads.

B And your emotions change too.

C What do you mean?

D You know – you go all moody sometimes.

A And sulky and argu... argumen... argumeti...

B Argumentative.

C But they can't help it – it's the hormones.

D Yeah, and I do still like my big sister.

A Of course, I like mine too.

B It's cool having an older brother sometimes.

C And my mum says that they grow out of this teen behaviour thing.

D Eventually.

A Right.

B That's that then.

C Yeah.

D Right.

INTERACTIVE FOLLOW UP ACTIVITIES

Questions

1) Why were the four children complaining about their older brothers and sisters?

   (Because they seemed to have changed for the worse; they were moody and argumentative etc.)

2) What caused the teenagers to change?

   (Hormones; growing up.)

3) What physical changes did the children mention?

   (Growing taller; putting on weight; deeper voices; greasy hair; spots.)

Getting the message

1) What can we learn from this sketch?

   (That teenagers change during puberty and that there are both physical and emotional changes; teenagers' hormones sometimes make them grumpy/moody etc – they can't always help it; their brothers and sisters need to be understanding; growing up is difficult!)

2) I'm going to read four statements about changes during growing up. Listen to them, then at the end you can vote for the one you agree with the most. *[Read the statements again.]*
   a. Life is easy for teenagers.
   b. Going through puberty is a difficult time.
   c. There's no excuse for being in a bad mood all the time.
   d. It won't happen to me.

Learning more

1) Do these changes only happen to teenagers.
   (No – puberty can start in primary school; it usually starts earlier in girls.)
2) Being a teenager isn't just about bad moods and spots: there's actually quite a lot to look forward to as well! Can you think of some good things about becoming a teenager?
   (Becoming more independent; developing new interests; earning a bit of money doing Saturday jobs; being given more responsibility; being able to make more choices for yourself, etc.)

NON-INTERACTIVE FOLLOW UP

Summary of the play

- The children noticed changes in their older brothers and sisters.
- Some changes were physical – like growing taller and heavier, getting spots and greasy hair or a deep voice.
- Some of the teenagers also changed emotionally – they were sometimes moody, sulky and argumentative, usually preferring to stay in their rooms.
- The children discussed this and found out it was all a normal part of growing up, and that chemicals in the body called hormones caused many of the changes.
- The children agreed that they still liked their older brothers and sisters, even if they were hard work sometimes.

Something to think about

1) Can moody teenagers always help their behaviour?
2) Do these changes happen to everyone?
3) How should we treat our older brothers and sisters?

Reflection

We all grow up; we all change. Treat teenagers and those younger who are going through puberty well; be patient and understanding with them – changing is hard and hormones often cause them to behave differently. Remember – it will all happen to you soon.

Prayer

Lord God, thank you that growing up is such an adventure. Help us to be kind and understanding towards our older brothers and sisters, especially those going through the difficult period of puberty with all its changes. Help us to remember that they can't always help what mood they are in. Let us be forgiving too, and please help us through our own teenage years. Amen.

1e Jobs Carried Out by People

Objective
To help children learn about the range of jobs carried out by people.

PSHE/Citizenship links
1e (The range of jobs carried out by people)

Props
Assembly book

Introduction
I'm reading from this book, but how did this book come to be made? You may be surprised at just how many people were involved in this book being here today and all the different jobs that were involved in it.

How a Book is Made

A book starts with an idea. Usually an author has the idea for a book, but sometimes it's someone else. Anyone can have an idea for a book. But whoever thinks of the book, it's written by an author. The author usually carries out some research first, such as checking facts and looking for information. He or she then writes a first draft of a book on a computer or typewriter. The first printout of the book is called a manuscript.

Books need to be published, so the author next sends the manuscript to a publishing company to see if they think the idea will make a good book. Sometimes the paper manuscript is packaged up and posted and sometimes it is put onto a disc and delivered but it can also be sent quickly by email. So postmen and women, and parcel delivery drivers may be involved at this stage. IT technicians will be working to make sure that computers and email systems are all operating smoothly too.

The manuscript will be read by a person called an editor. If the editor likes the book it will be taken to a publishing meeting. Several people at the publishers will discuss the idea and decide if the book will be published. It costs a lot of money to make a book so the publishers must make sure that the book will sell plenty of copies.

If the book is accepted, the manuscript has to be checked for mistakes and to see if the English makes sense. This is done by a proof-reader. The proof-reader checks the book very carefully and marks any changes that need to be made.

The editor will next discuss with the author things like illustration, design, and how the pages will look. At this stage, lots more people become involved in making the book. If the book needs pictures, these will be created by an illustrator. A designer will also work on the book, deciding how it will look, and what should go on the cover. The layout of the pages must be planned and the font for the text and the headings chosen.

The editor will help the author to make improvements to the way the book is written too, and make sure everything is clear for the reader. A person called a marketing manager will decide how to let people know that the book is being published and where they can buy it. The production manager will work out the cost of paper and printing for the book too.

When the illustrations are ready, the designer will put together some pages and send them to the editor and the author. Everyone will discuss the design and decide if it's right for the book. When all the pages are assembled they are printed out: these test pages are called proofs and they need to be checked very carefully for mistakes. After checking, the proofs are ready to go to the printer.

Large machines called printing presses print all of the pages for the book. They're usually quite noisy. Machine operators check that the machines are working properly and the printers check that the pages look exactly as they should. The pages then need to be trimmed to the right size, assembled in the right order and fixed together, or bound.

There are lots of ways of binding the pages of a book – sometimes they are glued, sometimes stapled and sometimes fixed with wire or plastic binders, like this book.

The books are now finished! They are put into boxes and delivered to the publishers. Delivery drivers will then take them around the country to shops, schools, libraries, internet booksellers and to people's houses. The sales manager at the publishing company will try to sell as many of the books as possible. Adverts will be placed and catalogues sent to schools, people will be employed to take telephone orders and to open and check the mail for postal orders. Someone will need to package the books to be sent through the post and do all the paperwork for the orders too.

So there we are – a lot of people are involved in making a book and a whole range of jobs need to be carried out before a book like this can be picked up and read by you or me.

INTERACTIVE FOLLOW UP ACTIVITIES

Questions
1) Why does it take so many different people to make a book?
   (There are so many different stages; it's complicated; many different skills are required.)
2) Which person does the author talk to the most? *(The editor.)*
3) Who are some of the people who work at a publishing company?
   (Editors, publishers, managers, sales people, marketing people, production managers, secretaries, office cleaners, etc.)

Getting the message

1) Lots of people are involved in a book – where does the money to pay them all come from?
2) Put your hand up when I mention someone who might have been involved in making this assembly book:

- editor ✓
- footballer
- chef
- proof-reader ✓
- hairdresser
- delivery driver ✓
- sales director ✓

- gardener
- designer ✓
- author ✓
- printer ✓
- marketing manager ✓
- vet
- plumber

Learning more

1) Name something else which lots of people are involved in making.
2) Are all the jobs involved in making a book important?

NON-INTERACTIVE FOLLOW UP

Summary of the assembly

- A lot of people are involved in making a book.
- The book is written by an author, who may have to carry out research.
- Authors send their books to publishing companies, where they are read by editors.
- Lots of other people work at publishers to help make the book a success: production managers, marketing teams, sales people, secretaries, assistants, etc.
- Illustrators and designers help to decide how the book will look.
- Printers create the pages and bind them together to make the finished book.
- Lots of people are involved with distributing, packaging, marketing and selling the book before it reaches the reader.
- All the jobs are important, and lots of different skills and knowledge are needed to make something that people will buy.

Something to think about

1) Would you like to do any of the jobs involved in making a book?
2) How can you make sure that you get a good job that you will enjoy when you are older?

Reflection

Making something like a book takes a long time, and involves lots of people all working together and working hard. Remember to work hard at school so that you can find a rewarding, enjoyable job when you leave school.

Prayer

Lord God, thank you for all the people that work hard to make books and all the other things that we can buy and enjoy. Help us to work hard at school so that we can learn and eventually we can go out to work, and find a job that we can really enjoy and do well at. Amen.

1f Looking After Money

Objective
To help children understand the benefits of saving money.

PSHE/Citizenship links
1f (Looking after money)

Preparation
This assembly is in the form of a short play script or sketch, and requires four volunteer children to read a part. The ideal actors would be four good readers from Y5 or Y6 with strong clear voices – any mixture of boys and girls. A short practice before the assembly would be very helpful, and each child will need a copy of the script.

Introduction
Everyone likes having money. As you get older, you'll probably be given more money – pocket money, money for birthdays and Christmas or perhaps for doing well at something. Some of you may even earn money by doing jobs. But what should you do with your money – spend or save? Today, we've got a short drama sketch, which explores that very question.

Play: Money, Money, Money

A   Hey – happy birthday.

B   Thanks.

C   Yeah, happy birthday.

D   Shame it's a school day.

A   You doing anything special then?

B   Not today – but I'm going to the new dry ski-slope on Saturday.

C   Cool – it's excellent there.

D   I wish I was going…

A   What presents have you got then?

B   I got a new CD player and a few books, and I got quite a lot of money too.

C   I much prefer getting money.

D   So do I – you can choose what you want to buy then.

A   So, how much did you get?

B   £60.

C   Sixty! Hey, can I be your friend?

D   You're friends already, you joker.

A   So come on – tell us what you're going to buy.

B   Well, I'm just going to get a couple of CDs.

C   Is that all?

D   You could buy loads with £60!

A   Aren't you going to spend it all, then?

B   No, I'm saving most of it.

C   Bo-o-rr-ing – My dad makes me do that sometimes when I get money.

D But that's not fair – it's your money not his.

A *[to B]* Have your parents told you to save some of your birthday money then?

B No, actually – it's my own decision.

C You must be saving up for something big like a TV.

D I couldn't wait – I would just spend it.

A So, are you saving up to buy something special then?

B Well, not really – I just think it's good to keep money for the future.

C But with £60 you could buy some really good clothes.

D Yeah, or some cool trainers.

A I'd buy a new PlayStation game and tons of sweets.

B I have thought about all that, but my older brother convinced me to save most of it.

C I know him – he's seventeen now isn't he?

D Yeah, I've seen him – he's a sixth former at the secondary school.

A So, what did he say to you?

B He didn't actually say anything – he's just always broke.

C Sounds like my big sister – "I wish I'd saved more money," she's always saying.

D So why do they need so much money?

A Yeah – what does your brother spend all his money on?

B Well, he wants driving lessons – they're really expensive, and he likes to go out for meals with his friends, and he needs a laptop for his A-level IT work, and some smart clothes for interviews too.

C But all that must cost a fortune.

D Surely your parents are helping him out?

A Mine would, I'm sure.

B Yeah, of course, they're paying for some things but he still wants to have his own money – he said he really regrets wasting loads of money on things when he was my age.

C I can see his point.

D I might start trying to save some of my pocket money.

A *[to B]* So, how much have you saved altogether then?

B I've got £238 in the bank.

C Hey! Can I be your friend?

INTERACTIVE FOLLOW UP ACTIVITIES

Questions

1) Whose idea was it to save most of the £60?
   (Child B's.)

2) Why did he/she decide to save the money?
   (His/her elder brother was always short of money for important things and wished he had saved more.)

3) What else might you need money for when you're 17?
   (School trips, bus money, snacks, holiday spending, music, a bike, haircuts, presents for other people, mobile phone, etc.)

Getting the message

1) What can we learn from this sketch?

   (That although spending money is fun, saving money is a good thing to do, as you are going to need more money when you grow up.)

2) Give these statements a thumbs up if you agree, and a thumbs down if you disagree.

   • Children should be able to spend their own money on whatever they want.

   • Saving money is a good idea.

   • When I'm older, I'll wish I'd saved more.

   • You should save so you can buy other people presents too.

   • The best thing to do is spend, spend, spend.

Learning more

1) Why is it a good idea to put money in a savings account or bank?

   (It can earn interest; it's safe there; you'll be less tempted to spend it; you can keep track of it.)

2) What do adults need to save money for?

NON-INTERACTIVE FOLLOW UP

Summary of the play

• One of the children was given £60 birthday money.

• He/she decided to save most of the money.

• The other children thought that spending it was a better idea.

• He/she noticed that his/her older brother, aged 17, was always short of money, especially for important things, and wished he had saved more when he was younger.

• The other children agreed that saving some money was a good idea, especially when they found out how much had been saved altogether.

Something to think about

1) Is it worth saving a bit of pocket money, even if you don't get much?

2) Should you save the money or should your parents do it for you?

3) In the future, do you think you will you look back and be glad you saved money, or sorry you didn't?

Reflection

Think about what you do with your money. Try to be responsible for your own money. Try to plan ahead – think of all the important things you will need money for in the future. Try to save regularly, even if it's just a little, and to put away some of the money you are given. One day, you'll be very glad you did.

Prayer

Lord God, thank you that you give us choices about what we do with our money. Help me to look after any money that I am given. Help me to be wise about saving for the future when I will really need money for important things. Please help me not to waste money on things that I don't really need or want, and also to be generous with my money. Amen.

2A TOPICAL ISSUES

Objective
To encourage children to discuss topical issues.

PSHE/Citizenship links
2a (Topical issues)

Props
(Not essential): a safety helmet

Introduction
In many ways the world is a much better place today than it was in the past. A long time ago, people had very little chance to choose what they wanted to do with their lives. Even last century, life was very dull for many people because there was so little opportunity to get an interesting job or to travel and visit new places or to spend money on all sorts of things that we take for granted today. So, what has caused the world to change for the better? Well, one of the causes is very simple: discussion. Listen to this example of what I mean...

TRUE STORY: STRONGER THAN STEEL

Do you know what Kevlar is? It's an amazing material, which is used for all sorts of important jobs. Safety helmets and crash helmets are often made out of Kevlar because it is incredibly strong. Kevlar consists of flexible fibres which can be moulded into any shape, but it is five times stronger than steel. That's why it is the material used to make bullet-proof vests.

Bullet-proof vests are worn by police officers and soldiers where guns are being used, and they have saved thousands of lives. Unlike steel, Kevlar is very light; it also does not rust. It is used in many other ways too: on car tyres, brake pads, spacecraft shells and boats. It is used to make parachutes, skis, underwater cables, suspension bridge cables and camping gear. It is used in buildings too, where something extra-strong is required.

Kevlar was invented by a woman called Stephanie Kwolek, about fifty years ago. Kevlar is a remarkable invention, not just because it is such a valuable material, but because Stephanie Kwolek had to overcome so many problems to discover it.

Stephanie was born in The United States of America in 1923. She was always interested in science, and when she left school she studied Chemistry at university in a city called Pittsburgh. Stephanie wanted to become a doctor but couldn't afford to pay for the training so she got a job with a large chemical company working in a laboratory doing research on new types of artificial fibres.

Stephanie enjoyed this work and did very well, but she was afraid that she would lose her job. The reason was that World War II had just ended and many men were returning from the army. Most scientists were men in those days and it was very difficult for a woman to find and keep a good job in a big chemical company. But Stephanie worked hard and proved that she was just as capable as any of the other scientists there, men or women.

Stephanie began to experiment with different chemicals to try to make new strong fibres, and she soon made lots of discoveries. After years of work, in 1966, she discovered how to make an incredibly strong new material. She called it Kevlar. Everyone at the company was astonished at this discovery and Kevlar soon became world famous. It was sold to people all over the world, earning millions of dollars for the company.

Stephanie Kwolek didn't stop there. She continued doing important research in her science lab and went on to discover lots more useful materials and processes. Eventually she received a number of awards and medals for her work and was recognised as one of the world's great scientists.

Today, in the 21st century, there are far more women scientists than there were in Stephanie Kwolek's day. More women have good, interesting jobs and opportunities to do all sorts of things that they were discouraged from doing in the past. One of the reasons for this change is that through the years, people have talked about the question of opportunities for women. Ideas have been discussed, people have argued and listened and questioned and talked about the issues and discussed them further.

And so, although it only happened slowly, things changed. The best ideas were accepted. People, by talking, agreed that women had every right to become scientists and get important jobs. People all over the world talked about discoveries like Kevlar and how useful they were. Through discussion, laws were made to stop discrimination and unfair decisions in companies and other places.

Of course, things are not perfect today – there are still women around the world who don't get the chances they deserve, but things are far better than they used to be, because people have spoken up and discussed and argued carefully for equal rights.

So the lesson we can learn from Stephanie Kwolek and Kevlar is simple: join in discussions; have your say about important issues; speak up for what you believe in – you never know – you might change the world.

INTERACTIVE FOLLOW UP ACTIVITIES

Questions
1) How has Kevlar saved people's lives?
   (It is used for bullet-proof vests and other safety equipment like crash helmets.)
2) Why was it so difficult for Stephanie Kwolek to invent something?
   (Very few women were given the chance to work in science labs; she had to work extra hard.)
3) Why is Kevlar so successful?
   (It's light, very strong, flexible and has a huge number of uses.)

Getting the message
1) What can we learn from this true story?
   (That women can be just as good at inventing as men; that hard work brings rewards; that talking can change things; that discussing something can even change the world.)

2) Show whether these statements are true or false by giving them a thumbs-up or thumbs-down:
   - Stephanie Kwolek only invented Kevlar. *(F)*
   - It was hard for Stephanie to find a good job as a scientist. *(T)*
   - There are fewer women scientists today than 50 years ago. *(F)*
   - Stephanie Kwolek's success probably helped other women to get good jobs. *(T)*
   - Unfair situations only change if people talk about them. *(T)*

Learning more

1) Did Stephanie Kwolek succeed just because she was clever, or did she have to work hard too?
2) Apart from discussion, how else do people try to change things?
   (Mention protests, use of force, violence, and also democracy – voting for change.)

NON-INTERACTIVE FOLLOW UP

Summary of the story

- Stephanie Kwolek was an American scientist born in the 1920s.
- After university she worked on research in a chemical laboratory.
- It was hard for Stephanie to keep her job because most scientists were men in those days.
- Stephanie created new fibres and made them into a material called Kevlar.
- Kevlar is 5 times stronger than steel but light and long-lasting.
- Kevlar became a huge success and is now used for bullet-proof vests and safety helmets among many other important uses.
- Stephanie received many awards and medals for her invention.
- There are more women scientists today, because of people like Stephanie Kwolek and because the question of equal opportunities for women has been discussed until people listened and accepted that it was right.

Something to think about

1) Why should you try to join in classroom discussions?
2) Is listening or talking more important?
3) How do you get to be famous like Stephanie Kwolek?

Reflection

Kevlar is a remarkable invention and Stephanie Kwolek is a remarkable woman. She had to work harder than everyone else just to keep her job but she succeeded in the end. She helped to make the world a fairer place. Try to join in classroom discussions about important questions so that you too can make things fair.

Prayer

Lord God, thank you for Stephanie Kwolek and for her great discovery of Kevlar. Thank you that millions of women today have more opportunities than they had in the past. Help us to join in discussions and to become interested in important issues like this. Amen.

2b Rules and Laws

Objective
To help children understand the need for rules and laws.

PSHE/Citizenship links
2b (Rules and laws)

Props
(Not essential): a large coin

Introduction
Our country has lots of rules and laws. There are laws about who can run the country, about buying and selling food, looking after animals, where you can drive, what you can say about other people and what's allowed on TV. There are rules about library books, football, how to play chess, visiting hours in hospital, dos and don'ts at the swimming pool and countless other things. But why do we have laws and rules? Listen to this story...

Story: The King's Head

Beaurocria is a small country situated in central Europe, near Austria and Slovakia. Well... actually, it isn't – it's not a real country at all. But, just for today, I'd like you to imagine that it is. Then you can find out what a terrible thing happened there sixteen and a half years ago...

The King of Beaurocria, Maximillian IX, was fed up. Really fed up. He'd spent another whole day listening to his ministers and advisers with their endless lists of complaints. By five o'clock, he couldn't stand it any longer.

"Stop!" he bellowed. "Stop, stop, stop, stop, stop. I don't want to hear any more."

"But your majesty," they said. "It is not we who are complaining."

"Well who is it then?"

"It is the people – the shopkeepers, the mothers, the soldiers, the farmers – well, everybody, really."

"And what are they complaining about?"

"They say they have to pay too much tax, they say they are always filling in forms, they say they are always waiting in queues, they say all the laws and rules of the land are driving them mad."

"Well, why are you telling me all this?"

"The people are saying that the king needs to do something, your majesty – only you have power over all these regulations."

"And have I?"

"You have."

"Well then let's do something about it – tonight I will think over the problem and tomorrow I will tell you what I have decided. Then perhaps we can have some peace around here."

And so the king of Beaurocria went away to his private study to think.

The next morning the king awoke early and, after a hearty breakfast, he called all of his ministers and advisers together.

"Now listen carefully. The people are complaining about the laws and rules of this land. They say there are too many. They say they are driving them mad. And I agree with them. Why do we need so many petty regulations and laws with endless paperwork and forms to fill in? I hate filling in forms!" (The King said this although he had never filled in a form in his life). "So, I have decided what will happen. I am going to do away with all the rules and laws of the land – get rid of them!" There was a gasp from the ministers. The advisers stood with open mouths in shock. Then one spoke up.

"But, your majesty, you cannot... there will be chaos, anarchy... it will not... cannot... work."

There were grumbles and nods of agreement from the others, but the king held up his hand and stopped them.

"Wait, wait – I have not finished. I am not a fool – I realise that we cannot take away all of the laws of the land, and so we shall keep two: No one is allowed to steal and no one is allowed to kill. Murderers and thieves will still go to jail, but all other laws are ended, as from midday today. Announce this to the people." The ministers and advisers thought about this but before they could answer, the king turned his back and walked away. That was all he had to say – it was done.

The following morning the king woke up late, and called his butler.

"Right, Strauss, what have you got lined up for me today?"

"Your majesty – a visit to the Royal Mint to see the brand new 50 Plenk coin – the one with your portrait on."

"Splendid!"

After breakfast, the king put on his best suit and went outside to his limousine, ready to visit the Royal Mint, across the city.

"Where is my driver?" he said. "Where is Kellmann?" The king's bodyguard was there.

"He's not here your majesty... he's still in bed."

"What! But it's ten o'clock!"

"Your butler went to his room but the driver said he can get up when he pleases now."

"Well, but, well... never mind – I'll drive the car!"

"I'm afraid you can't, your majesty," said the bodyguard. "Someone has parked a bus in front of the palace gates." The king was violet with rage.

"Very well then, I'll walk!" The king stomped off towards the gates, with his bodyguard close behind. Outside in the streets, there was a terrible racket. People were shouting and tooting their horns, and there were shoppers' cars parked everywhere: on the pavement, blocking roads – even in the middle of the street. A poor policeman was surrounded by a shouting mob. The king hurried on, towards the Royal Mint. Just as he was crossing the road, two boys sitting on the wall called out.

"Hey – look at him!"

"Watch this!" A tomato came winging through the air. It landed with a splat on one of the king's polished leather brogue shoes.

"You little scoundrels!" He turned to his bodyguard. "Arrest those two at once."

"I'm afraid I can't your majesty – they, err, haven't done anything against the law, you see."

The king was about to argue, when he thought better of it. Instead he turned and stormed on, walking faster than ever. It was a long way to the mint, and soon the king was hot and thirsty. After a few minutes, he spotted a cafe, and asked his bodyguard to buy him a large glass of wine. The man returned empty handed.

"Where's my wine?" said the king.

"Your majesty, they said that a glass of wine now costs 2000 plenks."

"What? Don't be ridiculous man – even I know that wine is only about 35 plenks a glass. There are plenty more cafes – we'll buy some elsewhere."

"But the owner said that wine now costs 2000 plenks everywhere – some places are charging even more."

The king was more furious than ever, but continued with his journey. He walked past teenagers writing graffiti, including a giant wall with *Down with the king!* and *The queen smells of old socks*; he walked past great piles of rubbish on the streets where the dustmen had taken the day off work, and through the park, which was full of sheep eating the grass on the football pitches and cows drinking from the ornamental pond. And finally, sweating, fuming and tomato-splattered, the king reached the Royal Mint. He was two hours late.

At the Royal Mint, the king sat down and rested. He was given a cool refreshing drink. Everything seemed in order here, and he began to feel much better. Then the new 50 plenk coin was presented to him.

"What's this!" boomed the king in horror. "This isn't my portrait!" The master of the mint stepped forward.

"I'm sorry, your majesty – I decided to put Elvis Presley on the new coin – I'm a big fan."

"But you can't do that – there are ru…"

"I can do what I like now," said the master of the mint, bowing politely.

It was early evening when the king arrived back at the palace – his mood was blacker than ever since he had paid for a taxi by handing over two gold rings and his best hat. A frantic gabbling throng of ministers and advisers was waiting for him.

"Your majesty – we will have to sell the palace – no one is paying any taxes."

That did it. The next day, all the laws were put back in place and everything returned to normal. Except one thing – the king made a new law: any child found throwing tomatoes at the king would be… well, it was too horrible to say.

INTERACTIVE FOLLOW UP ACTIVITIES

Questions

1) Who was complaining about laws and rules in Beaurocria?
   (Everyone.)

2) What was the result of the removal of all the laws?
   (Chaos – people did as they pleased.)

3) Why did the king change the laws back?
   (He realised that the laws were there for a reason.)

Getting the message

1) What can we learn from this story?

(That even though some of our laws and rules are unpopular, they are there to keep peace and order.)

2) Put your hand up when you agree with one of these statements:
   - Most rules and laws are good.
   - If you're not sure about a rule or law, it's best to ask.
   - There are too many rules.
   - People who break the law should be punished.
   - Rules and laws are the same for everybody.

Learning more

1) Name something that is against the law, e.g. stealing.
2) Can anyone think of a rule which helps keep you safe?

NON-INTERACTIVE FOLLOW UP

Summary of the story

- The people of Beaurocria were fed up with all the country's rules and laws.
- The king decided to do away with all the laws except two.
- The king had a lot of trouble getting to the Royal Mint because there were no longer any laws to stop people causing trouble.
- The king learnt that laws and rules were useful after all.
- All the old laws and rules were put back in place.

Something to think about

1) What are laws and rules for?
2) Should people who break rules have to face the consequences?
3) Do I know and understand the school rules?

Reflection

We all have to obey rules and laws. They are there to keep things fair, to keep us safe and to stop trouble. Rules are important – we need to understand them and try our best to keep to them.

Prayer

Lord God, thank you that we live in a country where the law of the land is designed to keep us safe. Please help us to obey the laws and rules that have been made for us. Help us to understand what they are for and that they keep us safe. Help us to say sorry if we break a rule. Amen.

2c ANTISOCIAL BEHAVIOUR

Objective
To help children understand the consequences of antisocial and aggressive behaviours.

PSHE/Citizenship links
2c (antisocial behaviour), 4d Racism, teasing and bullying

Props
(Not essential): a football

Introduction
Sometimes when you do something bad you get told off or punished. Occasionally you might get away with it. But if you continue to behave badly people will notice and they will remember. It may be that in the future you'll regret what you did. Today's story is about a boy who didn't realise the consequences of the trouble he'd caused when he was younger.

STORY: PAYING THE PRICE

Gary saw his chance. The tall lad with the fair hair was spending too long with his foot on the ball – he was showing off, trying to impress the selectors. Gary raced in from the side and hit the ground with a brutal sliding tackle. He just managed to catch the ball first before chopping away the fair-haired boy's legs from under him. There was a cry of pain as the tall lad flopped down onto the pitch dramatically. He would be all right, but Gary glanced at the ref just to be sure.

"Play on," waved the referee, sweeping his arm upwards.

"Yes!" thought Gary. "That was a great tackle – coaches always love players who get stuck in like that." And Gary was right. Standing on the touchline, watching the match, was a broad figure in a black tracksuit – none other than Colin Green, manager of Albion, a third division club. He was talking to his youth team coach, Sam Watson.

"That lad's the kind of footballer I like – hard as nails – he can run all day, tackle, and he's even got a nice touch on the ball. What's his name Sam?"

"Err let's have a look on the list... number 14... it's Gary Ellingford – he's a local lad too, fifteen years old."

"Right, let's see how he gets on in the second half."

The match was a special game that had been organised by Albion to choose their youth team for the coming season. All the local clubs and school teams had been watched by Albion's scouts, and their best young players had been invited to attend this match. Gary had been overjoyed when he was told that he had been selected to play in this trial game. It had been his dream to become a professional footballer, and this was his big chance. It wasn't going to be easy though – from the 22 players here, only a few would be signed up by the club.

Gary had played well in the first half, and felt sure that he would be noticed. Then, half way through the second half, things got even better. Gary was a defensive midfield player who didn't move forward to attack too often – his role was to stop the other team from scoring, but when his team won a corner, Gary decided to go up for it. He stood on the edge of the six-yard box and waited for the ball to be crossed. Gary was good at heading but he had a problem – he was being marked by a big defender. This lad was a lot taller than Gary so it would be almost impossible to out jump him.

But then Gary saw his chance. The defender took one step forward as the ball came over and, quick as a flash, Gary nipped behind him. Just as the defender was taking off to head the ball away, Gary gave him a shove in the lower back. The push was enough – Gary was able to rise above the defender with his own jump and then, in a wonderful moment, he thumped the ball with his head towards the goal. He watched with glee as it rocketed past the goalie's flailing arms and hit the back of the net.

There were whoops and cheers from his team mates and Gary clenched his fist hard. The ref had missed the push, and he had scored – it was even more than he had hoped for. Gary's side were now 2-1 up and there was only one more incident in the game. Gary was running out of defence with the ball when someone clipped one of his ankles from behind. Gary caught his left boot on the turf and fell hard, his face sliding on the cold mud of the pitch.

"Oi!" Gary screamed. It was the tall fair-haired lad – getting his revenge no doubt. Gary stood up quickly and confronted the boy, swearing and shoving him in the chest. The referee charged in between the two before further trouble could develop. He gave a free kick, but he also called Gary over and took out a yellow card.

"You can't do that, son – I'm booking you." Gary protested a little but decided to walk away – he didn't want to spoil his performance, not when the Albion selectors were watching. A few minutes later the final whistle blew – Gary's team had won and he had scored the winner!

Colin Green, the club manager, walked into the dressing room after the game.

"Well played lads – a good hard match. There were some fine performances out there too, and Mr Watson's made a lot of notes about all of you. I'm sure you're all desperate to know who has been selected. Right, what'll happen now is this: I'll sit down later today with Mr Watson, the youth team coach, and we'll discuss the game and make a list of those players we're interested in. In a couple of days, some of you will be receiving letters asking you to come back to the club to sign a contract to play for Albion. If you don't get a letter, that's it I'm afraid. So, it's waiting time next. Well done, everybody." He disappeared through the door, leaving all 22 players wondering and hoping.

The next few days were agony for Gary. He got up at 5am each morning and stared out of the living room window, anxious for the post to arrive. There was no letter on Monday, and there was nothing on Tuesday either. The week passed and there wasn't any post for Gary. He was devastated. On Friday, back at school, he asked Mr Hill, his PE teacher about the letter.

"If you haven't heard by now, Gary, I'm afraid that's it – I'm really sorry."

"But I played great in the trials – I even scored the winner."

"I know you did Gary – I spoke to Albion's manager on Monday."

"What, Mr Green?"

"Yes, he called me with a few questions about you. He said you'd done very well in the game."

"So, why haven't I been picked?"

"Gary – come and sit down in the classroom and we'll talk about this."

Mr Hill looked strangely sad as he drew up his chair opposite Gary's.

"Right, Mr Green said that you'd played well, but he did notice a couple of things in the match."

"What, the yellow card you mean?"

"And a few bad fouls, and when you pushed the defender for the goal."

"Oh, I see."

"But that wasn't actually the reason, Gary, it was... well, word had got through to him from somewhere that you've regularly been in trouble. He phoned and asked me about the court cases, Gary – I had to tell him."

"But, that's nothing to do with football."

"Maybe, but the manager wants players with the right character, not people who might cause trouble – you've been accused of damaging property, assault, theft and racial abuse Gary. There are a lot of black players at Albion, you know."

"This isn't fair, Mr Hill."

"Gary, I warned you, the police warned you and your parents warned you that you couldn't carry on with that behaviour – now you've discovered the consequences."

Gary trudged home with tears in his eyes, his shoulders slumped.

What happened to Gary? Well, he never did hear from Albion, but he did become a professional footballer with another club. After that day with Mr Hill in the classroom, he changed his ways – he stopped stealing and vandalising, he stopped taunting and bullying and being a racist. He joined an amateur football team and was spotted by a scout from a second division club. Of course, Gary still gets a few yellow cards now and again – but that's all – he knows the consequences.

INTERACTIVE FOLLOW UP ACTIVITIES

Questions

1) Why was Gary's football match so special?

   (It was a game where a professional team were choosing players to join their club.)

2) Why didn't Gary get selected for Albion?

   (The manager found out that he had been in trouble with the police and courts.)

3) What happened to Gary?

   (He changed his ways, stopped getting into trouble and became a professional footballer.)

Getting the message

1) What can we learn from this story?

   (That there are consequences to serious bad behaviour; people who misbehave get a bad name, and this gets around.)

2) Give each of these behaviours a score, by holding up fingers: 1 finger = not too bad, 5 fingers = bad, 10 fingers = very serious bad behaviour.
- graffiti
- bullying
- fighting
- damaging property
- stealing
- using racist names

Learning more
1) What other consequences are there for antisocial and aggressive behaviours?
2) How can people who do this be stopped?

NON-INTERACTIVE FOLLOW UP

Summary of the story
- Gary was a good footballer, aged 15.
- He was invited to a trial match with a professional club called Albion.
- He did well in the game and scored a goal.
- The manager noticed Gary and thought he'd done well.
- Gary wasn't chosen for the club and was very disappointed.
- Gary's PE teacher told him it was because he'd previously been in too much trouble with the police.
- Gary stopped misbehaving and became a professional footballer.

Something to think about
1) Do you have a good name for your behaviour or a bad name?
2) What are the consequences of antisocial and aggressive behaviours?

Reflection
Think about Gary, who nearly lost a great chance to live his dream because of his bad behaviour. Remember that word gets around and that people can soon get a bad reputation. Remember that bullying and racism are wrong. Treat others in the way that you would like to be treated yourself.

Prayer
Lord God, please help us to behave well towards each other – to avoid antisocial behaviour and aggression. Help us to realise that these behaviours have consequences that go beyond punishment. Thank you that it's possible to mend our ways if we've been bad in the past, and to alter the way we behave. Please help us to give ourselves a good name. Amen.

2D RESPONSIBILITIES, RIGHTS AND DUTIES

Objective
To help children understand how we're all responsible for looking after our planet.

PSHE/Citizenship links
2d (Responsibilities, rights and duties)

Props
None

Introduction
Today's assembly starts with a poem written by Brian Patten called *The Newcomer*. It's a kind of mystery poem and I'd like you to listen to it carefully and try to work out what it's about.

POEM: THE NEWCOMER

"There's something new in the river,"
The fish said as it swam,
"It's got no scales, no fins, no gills,
And ignores the impassable dam."

"There's something new in the trees,"
I heard a bloated thrush sing,
"It's got no beak, no claws, no feathers,
And not even the ghost of a wing."

"There's something new in the warren,"
The rabbit said to the doe,
"It's got no fur, no eyes, no paws,
Yet digs deeper than we can go."

"There's something new in the whiteness,"
Said the snow-bright polar bear,
"I saw its shadow on a glacier
But it left no foot-prints there."

Throughout the animal kingdom
The news was spreading fast –

No beak no claws no feathers
No scales no fur no gills,
It lives in the trees and the water,
In the earth and the snow and the hills,
And it kills and it kills and it kills.   *Brian Patten*

[Poem published in *Gargling with Jelly*, Brian Patten, Puffin Books 1986.]

So, what is the newcomer? Before you answer – let's look at the clues:

1) It's found in water, in trees, in the ground and in snow.
2) It's got no beak or claws or fur or any kind of body at all.
3) It can go places where animals can't go.
4) It kills things.

Hands up – who knows what it is? *(Answer: pollution)*

Pollution is often invisible and it can go places where animals can't. Pollution is made up of chemicals, which can affect trees and plants, get into water and soil and travel through the air. Pollution is sometimes invisible too –poisonous gases often can't be seen. And because pollution often does contain poisons, it kills animals.

The poem is called *The Newcomer* because animals have been around for thousands of years but it is only in the last two hundred years that people have really started causing widespread pollution. To the ancient earth, it is something new – and something deadly.

So how do we cause so much pollution? Well, nearly everything that human beings do causes pollution. Pollution isn't just from car exhausts and smoky chimneys. All the things around us have been manufactured and almost every time people make things, the factories where they are made cause pollution. The shops are full of things we like to buy, but making these causes pollution. Heating our houses and schools causes pollution and so does cooking food. Every time something is transported, that causes pollution. And then there's all the waste we produce: packaging, plastic bags, cans and bottles, old fridges and cookers by the million.

There is no easy answer to pollution – it happens simply because there are so many people living in the world and we all like to own things. But we can stop polluting our rivers and trees and countryside and we can stop animals dying by using technology to keep pollution down to a minimum and by being careful about the things we buy and do. It is everyone's responsibility to look after our home – the planet Earth: after all, it's the only home we've got.

INTERACTIVE FOLLOW UP ACTIVITIES

Questions
1) Where did the newcomer come from?
   (Pollution – from factories, cars, homes, rubbish etc.)
2) Who is responsible for animals being killed?
   (People who cause pollution – everybody!)
3) Why were the animals mystified by the newcomer?
   (Because pollution is often invisible or it seems to have no 'body'.)

Getting the message
1) What can we learn from this poem?
   (That pollution can kill animals; that many things cause pollution; it cannot easily be seen; we're all responsible for pollution.)

2) Put your thumb up if I say a true statement and thumb down if I say a false statement:
- Burning things causes pollution. *(T)*
- Making electricity usually causes pollution. *(T)*
- Most rivers in Britain are now full of pollution, which kills fish.
  (F – explain that new laws have actually 'cleaned up' rivers.)
- Dropping litter causes pollution. *(T)*

Learning more
1) Name something that you can do to cut down pollution.
2) Cars cause a lot of pollution – how does this affect people in cities?

NON-INTERACTIVE FOLLOW UP

Summary of the poem
- The animals have noticed that there is a strange newcomer in their midst.
- It can be found in rivers, in trees, in the ground, and in the snow.
- The newcomer has no body and cannot easily be seen.
- Wherever it goes the newcomer kills and kills.
- The newcomer is pollution.

Something to think about
1) Why is it everyone's responsibility to keep pollution down to a minimum?
2) What can I do to stop pollution killing animals?

Reflection
We're all responsible for pollution because making the things we like causes pollution. We need to think about the things that cause a lot of pollution and try to lead cleaner, greener lives or we will spoil our planet.

Prayer
Lord God, thank you for the wonderful world that we live in. Please help us to find ways to cut down pollution and to protect our precious planet Earth and all the plants and animals that we share it with. Help us all to be responsible. Amen.

2E MORAL ISSUES

Objective
To help children reflect on spiritual, moral, social and cultural issues.

PSHE/Citizenship links
2e (spiritual, moral, social and cultural issues)

Props
(Not essential): a cardboard box

Introduction
When you grow up and leave school, I'm sure that you would like to get a good job, earn plenty of money and live in a nice house. But what if someone told you that you weren't allowed to have a good job and that it was against the law for you to have a decent house? What if you were told that you had to live in a home made of old boxes? For over fifty years this happened to millions of people.

TRUE STORY: NELSON MANDELA BEATS APARTHEID

Samuel and Jack were both twenty years old. Jack lived in a large house with a swimming pool and servants. Jack [samuel] lived in a small low house built of mud bricks, corrugated iron and cardboard boxes. Samuel was not allowed to visit Jack or even to go into the town where he lived.

Jack worked in a smart office, in a tall building with air conditioning. He had a good job and earned a lot of money. Samuel swept the road outside the building where Jack worked. He wasn't allowed in the building and he earned barely enough money for food. Samuel was as clever and as hard working as Jack, but he wasn't allowed a good job in an office: the law said so.

Jack sometimes called in at the post office round the corner to buy a drink and then went to sit in the park near his offices at lunchtime. Samuel sometimes went in the same post office to post a letter, but he had to go in a different doorway at the side of the building. Samuel would have liked to sit in the park sometimes too, but he wasn't allowed in there – the park was only for people like Jack.

After a long day at work, Jack drove his Mercedes home, past the big new school where his children were taught. Samuel had to walk a long way to catch a bus that took him a long, long way out of town, into the dusty dry village where he lived, among the rusty shacks. Samuel wasn't even allowed on a good bus like Jack would have been – he had to catch an old, slow, dirty bus that stopped endlessly.

Samuel's children went to a school out of town. It had huge classes of over sixty children and hardly any books or equipment. Samuel's children were not allowed to go to the smart new school that Jack's children went to.

How could all this happen? Is this really true? Yes, this happened to many millions of people just like Jack and Samuel. But how, you might ask. It happened because Samuel was black and Jack was white. It happened right up until the 1980s, in South Africa.

39

The laws, which treated black and white people so differently, were called apartheid, which means 'apartness'. Quite simply, and until quite recently, the country was ruled by a white government, which kept blacks and whites apart. They were not allowed to live in the same areas, whites were not allowed to marry blacks, and blacks and Asians were banned from all sorts of areas of life. White people were given all the best jobs and owned nearly all the land. Black people were made to do all the dirty boring jobs and earned on average 14 times less than whites.

Black people were not allowed to vote and were not allowed to travel into white areas. They had separate buses, train carriages, parks, hospitals, schools, shops, and even beaches. Of course, the whites had the best of all of these. In some places separate foot bridges were built so that white South Africans would not have to walk next to people with dark skin.

This system was very cruel and wrong. It discriminated against people just because of the colour of their skin. Today, we call this racism, but because it was kept in place by the country's government, it continued in South Africa for many years.

In 1978, there were 19 million black people in South Africa but only 4.5 million whites. Naturally the black people wanted to change apartheid and get a fair deal in their country but because they were not allowed to vote, they could not change the government. Many blacks protested but the white police dealt severely with demonstrators: there were fines, imprisonments and whippings every day.

Some black South Africans tried to organise large rallies to protest against the government – some of the leaders of this movement made speeches calling for the blacks to fight the whites to gain their freedom. But the government called in soldiers to break up these gatherings, and violence often broke out – in 1960, 69 people were killed at a place called Sharpeville – this became known as the Sharpeville Massacre. The black leaders of these protests were arrested by the police and given harsh treatment: torture, life imprisonment and even death sentences.

One of these leaders was called Nelson Mandela. Nelson was a black South African, born in 1918, who was the son of a tribal chieftain. He had been given a good education, in the days before the apartheid laws were passed and he became a lawyer in the 1940s. Nelson passionately believed that apartheid was wrong. He wanted to see black South Africans treated fairly and given the same chance as whites so he became involved in politics.

Nelson Mandela was a clever leader and a powerful speaker, and the white police arrested him a number of times for speaking out against the white authorities. In 1964 he was brought to trial and sentenced to life imprisonment for plotting to overthrow the government. He was taken to a high security jail on Robben Island just off the coast. Prisoners were put here to stop them escaping. Nelson was treated cruelly in this place – shut off from the world and given hard labour.

Nelson Mandela was locked up for 18 years in this dreadful prison, but he was not forgotten. The world knew about apartheid and it knew about Nelson Mandela. To many people he was a great hero, brave enough to speak out against injustice. People from many different countries began to campaign for Nelson to be released and for the South African government to end apartheid. At first the country's white leaders took no notice of these protests but as the years passed, the campaigns grew stronger and stronger.

Nelson Mandela became a symbol of the fight for equal rights for the millions of blacks in his country. He could have been released from jail by apologising to the government and saying that he had been wrong to protest, but he refused. In the 1970s and 1980s television pictures were beamed around the world showing how cruelly blacks were being treated and soon the governments of powerful nations like Britain and America were calling for apartheid in South Africa to change.

Many people stopped buying produce from South Africa, like fruit, and some countries refused to sell goods to the country. South African sports teams were banned from competing in international matches. Songs were released calling for change. Pressure was growing.

Nelson Mandela was eventually released from jail in 1990: he had been locked up for over a quarter of a century altogether in various prisons. He looked old and frail but his mind was still strong. The world next demanded that there should be proper, fair elections in South Africa for the first time – with everyone, black or white – allowed to vote. In 1994 this finally happened. Millions of blacks queued excitedly in the blazing heat to choose a new leader for their country. There was only one man who could possibly win this historic election.

Nelson Mandela was elected President of South Africa in 1994, the country's first black leader. He quickly set about changing the laws and making the country a fairer place for blacks. At long last Samuel was given the same opportunities as Jack. Many leaders in the new President's position would have then treated the white people as badly as they had treated the blacks. But Nelson Mandela did not do this. He wanted South Africa to become a free and fair nation for everyone to enjoy. That is why he is a great man.

INTERACTIVE FOLLOW UP ACTIVITIES

Questions
1) Why did Jack and Samuel not have the same chances in life at first?
   (Because the apartheid system in South Africa stopped blacks from being treated fairly.)
2) Why did Nelson Mandela get put in jail?
   (For protesting against apartheid.)
3) What made the South African government change?
   (Pressure from people and other countries around the world.)

Getting the message
1) What can we learn from this amazing true story?
   (Not to give up; to speak up for what you believe in; to stand up for a fair deal for all races and cultures etc.)
2) Nelson Mandela became President of South Africa because people voted for him in an election. Listen to these statements, then at the end you can vote for the one you agree with the most. [Read the statements again.]
   a. It's best if only the very rich and important people in a country vote.
   b. It's important for people to use their vote to choose their own leaders.
   c. All people should be made to vote.
   d. Voting is a waste of time.

Learning more

1) Why is Nelson Mandela regarded as a hero all over the world and not just in South Africa?
2) Do we have racism and discrimination in Britain?

NON-INTERACTIVE FOLLOW UP

Summary of the story

- For many years South Africa was ruled by white people who treated black people very badly.
- The government ran a system called apartheid, which kept black and white people apart.
- White people were allowed to have better homes, jobs, more money, better schools, hospitals and transport as well as many other advantages.
- Many blacks protested about these laws but they were often arrested, tortured and imprisoned for this.
- Nelson Mandela was a black leader in the 1960s, who was jailed for telling blacks to oppose apartheid.
- Mandela spent 28 years in various prisons before being released in 1990, when people and governments all over the world called for South Africa to change.
- Mandela became the country's first president in 1994, after proper elections allowed blacks to vote.

Something to think about

1) Sometimes when things seem hopeless for us, we can recall Nelson Mandela's amazing change from prisoner to world leader.
2) What would have happened if the black people had not bothered to vote when they finally got the chance?

Reflection

We're all treated badly sometimes and life does seem unfair on some days. But when you're feeling sorry for yourself, remember what life was like for black children in South Africa in the 1970s: hard, empty, cruel and full of poverty. Remember Nelson Mandela's bravery in standing up for what was right, too.

Prayer

Lord God, help us to treat everyone with fairness, whatever the colour of their skin, or however they talk, or whatever they look like. Help us to remember the poor blacks of South Africa who suffered years of cruelty and poverty and help us to recall the bravery of the man who helped to change things, Nelson Mandela. Thank you for his example to us all. Amen.

2f RESOLVING DIFFERENCES

Objective
To help children understand how differences can be resolved.

PSHE/Citizenship links
2f (Resolving differences)

Props
(None)

Introduction
It's a fact that every person in the world is unique. That means nobody is the same as another person. Every human being is different from every single other one: we have different looks, different personalities, different thoughts and ideas and different ways of doing things. This makes the world a very interesting place, but it also means that there are lots of arguments, disagreements, disputes and confrontations. So, how do we deal with them?

RESOLVING DIFFERENCES – BIG AND SMALL

It has probably happened to most of you: there's one chocolate biscuit left in the tin and both you and your brother want it. He grabs for it, so do you. There's an argument and you both get told off. Resolving this problem is easy – just snap the biscuit in half – but there are other differences at home that are harder to sort out.

Bed times are often an issue at home. You want to stay up a bit later to watch a TV programme. Your parents say "No". But all your friends watch it – or so you say – it's not fair. A few minutes won't make any difference. But your parents insist – they don't like the programme anyway – there is sometimes bad language in it – and it's a school day tomorrow: you need to be up early. So how do we resolve this one?

There is a famous book written for adults called *To Kill a Mockingbird*. It was written by the American author, Harper Lee. In the book, a girl called Scout is talking to her father, a wise man called Atticus, about getting into arguments. "What you need to do is walk around in the other man's shoes," says Atticus. What he means is, try to see the situation from the other person's point of view. So, back to the bed time dispute: let's try to see it from the parents' point of view.

Parents do want the best for their children, and they know that sleep is very important. You won't concentrate properly at school if you're tired from lack of sleep. Also, no one can argue that hearing bad language is a good thing. And perhaps your parents have had a long tiring day at work and just want a bit of peace and quiet away from children. Oh, and before you complain about them seeing the situation from your point of view, remember that they were children once and probably went through the same dispute with their parents!

Another difference that often arises at home is about helping around the house: tidying up, clearing away in the kitchen, sorting out washing and so on. Most children don't like doing it, but think – if you do help, you're much more likely to be listened to when you want your parents to help you. You can perhaps reach a deal, where you agree to do certain jobs regularly without having to be asked – perhaps the ones which you don't mind doing too much. If it becomes a habit then it will be easy for you. Remember again to see this from the point of view of other people in your home – it simply isn't fair if they have to do all the household jobs.

Differences between people often arise at school. There are a number of questions which crop up in many schools regularly: who should be allowed to go for dinners first? What should be done about games of football taking over the playground in winter? Should primary school children wear uniform? For each of these questions there are always at least two sides: two groups of people who have different views. For example, there are people who think school uniform is a good idea and those who don't. Each side needs to think carefully about the reasons why they might be right and to tell these to the other side. The people who disagree need to listen to each other so that they have a chance to understand the arguments on both sides.

This happens on a bigger scale in towns and cities. In a local town there might be all sorts of problems to be resolved such as: should parking in the town centre be free? Who should pay for the Christmas lights? Should a new petrol station be built next to the park? Just as before, the people who have different viewpoints need to present a good case for their argument – perhaps write it down so others can read it. They need to listen to what the general public think – maybe there will be a poll, with shoppers in the street asked to give their opinions. Or perhaps an article in the local newspaper will set out the two arguments for and against and then people can write letters to the paper. Maybe a local radio phone-in would help, or there might be a public meeting.

In each case, people need to listen to the viewpoints of each side, to consider different alternatives and explain the choices carefully, so everyone understands the reasons for a particular view. Often people get angry about decisions made by councils or local authorities, because they don't understand the background to the issue. The fairest way to solve many of these differences is by voting, so everyone can affect the result.

Differences between people happen on a bigger scale too. Governments have to sort out disputes about very big questions such as should Britain give up pounds and pence and start using the Euro as its currency? Or there are situations like the problems of Northern Ireland, where some people think that the people should be part of the Republic of Ireland and some people think they should be part of the UK.

There are huge disputes right across the world too. Sometimes whole countries seem to disagree and, sadly, these conflicts can lead to war. Israel has had a major difference with the Palestinian people for over 50 years. The recent War in Iraq also showed that big powerful countries cannot always resolve their differences peacefully.

But wars don't just 'happen'. Beforehand there are usually talks between the sides to try to avoid fighting. Alternatives are considered before making decisions, and often both sides try very hard to explain the different choices that are possible.

But, whether it's two children arguing over a biscuit, or two presidents arguing over a country, we can all learn from Atticus – we need to "walk around in the other man's shoes" before we say we are right.

44

INTERACTIVE FOLLOW UP ACTIVITIES

Questions

1) Why are there so many differences between people?
   (Because people are different.)
2) What does 'walking around in the other man's shoes' mean?
   (Try to see things from the other person's point of view.)
3) What happens sometimes when whole countries can't agree on something?
   (War.)

Getting the message

1) How can people resolve differences?
   (Listening to each other; explaining carefully; looking at alternatives; voting; sharing, etc.)
2) Imagine two friends are having a disagreement about whether they should go to Cornwall for their holidays. Which of these statements will help to settle the argument? Put your hand up or down for each one:
   - Let's give it a try – we won't know until we've been there.
   - You chose last year so it must be my turn to choose.
   - Let's find out more about Cornwall before we decide.
   - It sounds nice.
   - I've heard it's rubbish, so let's go somewhere else.
   - Let's talk to a few people who've been there.

Learning more

1) If you let the other person decide in a disagreement – how might that benefit you?
2) How do you settle family disputes at home?

NON-INTERACTIVE FOLLOW UP

Summary of the assembly

- All people are different so it is not surprising that people often disagree with each other.
- Disagreements in the home are sometimes easy to sort out and sometimes not.
- We need to try to see things from the other person's point of view.
- Differences at school can be resolved through discussion, sharing ideas, looking at alternatives and making decisions.
- Bigger questions like those made by councils and governments are also discussed and then they're voted on.
- If we don't learn how to sort out small differences then big ones can even lead to terrible results like war.

Something to think about

1) How can you 'walk around in the other man's shoes'?
2) Which is more important in a disagreement, talking or listening?

Reflection

We all have disagreements and there are times when we are right and times when the other person is right. Usually though, there is no simple right and wrong in these situations. What we need to do is to listen to the other person's point of view and try to understand it, then try to explain what we think, as carefully as possible. If you do this, you can often sort things out.

Prayer

Lord God, thank you that you gave us the ability to explain our point of view, and ears to hear what others have to say. Please help us to settle our differences. Help us to be good listeners and especially to try to understand the other person's point of view. Help governments and nations to settle their disputes across the world so that we can live in peace. Amen.

2G DEMOCRACY

Objective
To help children understand what democracy is and why it is important.

PSHE/Citizenship links
2g (What democracy is)

Props
(Not essential): a woolly hat

Introduction
Just imagine if the government passed a new law in parliament, which said that everyone had to wear a woolly hat every day, winter and summer *(hold up the hat)*. Well, it would drive us round the bend. If that did happen, then people would demand an election and vote for a different government right away. Of course, that's a very silly example and would never really happen, but it shows that ordinary people can have a say in who runs the country by voting – this is called democracy.

TRUE STORY: EMMELINE PANKHURST AND THE SUFFRAGETTES

One hundred years ago, life in Britain was very different. There were virtually no cars on the road, there were no aircraft in the skies and people looked, dressed and spoke in ways that would seem a little strange to us. There was another difference too: men and women were not treated equally in almost any way. Women, for example were not allowed to own property, such as houses. They could not become Members of Parliament and they weren't even allowed to vote in elections. Men decided everything.

Many people disagreed with this state of affairs and wanted to see things change. One of these was a woman called Emmeline Pankhurst. Emmeline was a clever, strong-willed and caring woman who grew up in Manchester in Victorian times. In those days, people who were unemployed or too poor to pay their bills were sent to a place called a workhouse. These were often dreadful places: people were treated like slaves, working long hours in filthy conditions, and watched over by cruel overseers.

Emmeline used to visit workhouses and she was shocked to see the misery and suffering of the people working there, especially women. She believed that the only way for this situation to change was for women to be able to vote so that they could elect a government that would stop people suffering in workhouses. So Emmeline campaigned for votes for women: she wrote letters to MPs, organised meetings, spoke to people and gave talks or lectures. But nothing changed. The newspapers didn't even take much notice of Emmeline and her supporters.

In 1905, Emmeline's daughter Christabel, who was then 25, went to a meeting in London. An important politician called Sir Edward Grey was giving a speech. As he was talking, Christabel and her friend Annie Kenney shouted out, "Will the Government give votes to women?" They kept on shouting and were eventually arrested by the police and fined five shillings each. The women refused to pay and were sent to prison. Suddenly the newspapers were interested in this story. They called Emmeline, Christabel and their supporters 'suffragettes'.

Emmeline Pankhurst realised that taking direct action like this was the only way to get people to take notice of what they were saying. The suffragettes began to break the law so that people would start talking about changing the law to allow women to vote. They smashed windows, blocked roads, and chained themselves to railings. One woman was killed when she threw herself under the King's horse at a race meeting. The police acted quickly and many women were sent to prison – Emmeline herself was gaoled 13 times. Some of the suffragettes went on hunger strike in prison, refusing anything to eat, and were force-fed by officers.

But still the law did not change and still women could not vote. Then, in 1914, World War I broke out. Millions of British soldiers were sent to France and Belgium to fight the Germans. Emmeline Pankhurst did a very wise thing. She told her supporters to stop protesting and to start helping their country in this time of national crisis.

Suddenly, with so many men sent away to fight, women found themselves doing important jobs that they had never had the chance to do before: they made guns in factories, they drove ambulances and worked on farms. People began to notice this important hard work and came to realise that women could easily do things that they thought could only be done by men.

After the war, opinion began to change, and the suffragette movement began to gain more and more support, even from powerful politicians. Finally, in 1928, Parliament agreed to change the law and allow women to vote. Emmeline Pankhurst, now 70 years old, died the same year. She had done it.

So, now we live in a properly democratic country – every adult is allowed to vote. This means that ordinary people – men and women – can choose who they want in charge. It's a very important right, one that many brave people have fought long and hard for.

INTERACTIVE FOLLOW UP ACTIVITIES

Questions

1) Why did Emmeline Pankhurst tell women to cause trouble?

   (So people would take notice of her campaign for women's votes.)

2) Why weren't women allowed to vote?

   (Men thought that women couldn't do as much and didn't work as hard.)

3) What changed people's views about women?

   (How well they did jobs during the First World War.)

Getting the message

1) What can we learn from this true story?

   (That democracy is important. Sometimes you have to stand up for something you believe in and work long and hard to achieve it.)

2) Put your hand up when you hear a true statement about democracy:
   - Democracy means people can have a say in something by voting. *(T)*
   - Britain has always had democracy. *(F)*
   - Children can vote in elections. *(F)*
   - Some people don't vote because they can't be bothered. *(T)*
   - Adults can vote in local elections to choose who is on local councils. *(T)*

Learning more

1) Does every country around the world have democracy?
2) Why is it important to vote?

NON-INTERACTIVE FOLLOW UP

Summary of the story

- Emmeline Pankhurst began to campaign for women's votes about 100 years ago.
- She was shocked at how badly women were treated in workhouses.
- Her daughter was arrested and put in prison for interrupting a political meeting.
- Emmeline and her supporters were called suffragettes.
- Many suffragettes broke the law to get noticed and were put in prison.
- When World War I broke out, Emmeline told women to help with the war effort.
- People saw that women could do heavy, difficult, important jobs just as well as men.
- Women were given the vote in 1928, the year Emmeline Pankhurst died.

Something to think about

1) Why is voting important?
2) Why did the suffragettes fight so hard for it?

Reflection

Emmeline Pankhurst and the suffragettes were brave, remarkable women because they suffered for something that they believed in. Remember their struggle and how important democracy is.

Prayer

Lord God, help us to remember brave people who fought for democracy – for the right to vote and to stop cruelty and suffering. Thank you that women can now vote and that there are no more workhouses. Amen.

2h Voluntary Groups

Objective
To help children learn about the role of voluntary groups in the UK.

PSHE/Citizenship links
2h (Voluntary, community and pressure groups)

Props
(Not essential): a paperback book

Introduction
I wonder if you've got some old books at home that you never look at any more. Well maybe you could do some good with them. Maybe they could even help someone who can't walk to move around. Listen to this true story to find out how.

True Story: Sue Ryder Care

Edgar is 83 years old. His lungs are very weak and he gets out of breath quickly. Edgar can move around but he cannot walk more than a couple of paces without having to sit down and rest. He finds this very frustrating, especially because he loves being outside most of all. Edgar spent most of his life working on a farm and he hates being stuck indoors, particularly as he has to spend most of his time just sitting down in a chair. He doesn't like watching TV and he finds reading difficult because his eyes are weak.

Edgar's favourite pastime is to go around the large garden at the back of the hall where he lives, looking at the flowers and stopping to feed the birds, and enjoy the view of the hills. Of course, Edgar can't do this by himself – he needs to be pushed in a wheelchair by someone else.

Edgar lives in a special home for elderly people in Lancashire, which is run by Sue Ryder Care, a charity. Lots of volunteers go there to help the nurses. It's these people who help Edgar to get out into the garden, and chat to him. Edgar loves talking about the old days on the farm, when he was in charge of the horses before there were any tractors. The volunteers love to listen to Edgar too – they all agree that his stories are very funny.

Edgar is very grateful for the way he's looked after by the Sue Ryder Care Centre. He sometimes wonders what would become of him if this charity didn't exist and if there were no volunteers to help him move about. Like all the other residents in the Care Centre, he's very grateful to the person who started it all.

Sue Ryder was born in 1923. When she was a young woman, the Second World War broke out and Sue volunteered to become a first aid nurse. She joined something called the Special Operations Executive – an organisation that carried out secret work behind enemy lines. Sue was sent to Poland where she helped secret agents to fight the Nazis. It was very dangerous work, and many of the brave people that Sue got to know were killed in action.

After the war ended, there were millions of people in Europe whose homes had been bombed or who had been kept in prisons or who had lost their families in the fighting. Everywhere there were poor, lonely, injured, sick and homeless men, women and children.

50

Sue Ryder desperately wanted to do something to help these people. At first she joined international relief agencies but then began to raise money herself to help people in hospitals and among the bombed ruins.

In 1953, Sue Ryder registered a charity called the Living Memorial, and set up headquarters in Suffolk. She met lots of other people who wanted to help those in need and soon the charity grew. It then became known as the Sue Ryder Foundation, and with all the money that was being raised by donations the charity began to open Care homes both in Britain and abroad. The organisation went on growing and helping more and more people all over the world. Sue Ryder's wonderful work was recognised and the Queen gave her the title of Lady Ryder. Sue Ryder died in 2000, but the movement she started is stronger than ever.

Today, Sue Ryder Care, as the charity is known, runs 18 Care Centres, like Edgar's. It helps people with disabilities and people with serious diseases. Like other charities, it employs people to keep it running smoothly and it relies on hundreds of volunteer helpers to carry out its work – ordinary people who give up their time to help others.

Sue Ryder Care Homes are very expensive places to run too – there are buildings to buy and maintain, furniture and beds to replace, heating and electricity bills, food to buy, wages to pay, special equipment to supply – the list is endless. The charity depends entirely on donations and fund-raising to provide all this money. A lot of money comes from Sue Ryder shops – you may have seen these in the high street of towns and cities. There are 430 of these shops altogether, run once again by volunteers. The shops sell all sorts of things which people have given to them: clothes, CDs, household goods, toys and books.

So, if you do have any old books, which you're not going to read, lying around at home, perhaps you could take them down to your local Sue Ryder shop. Or you could take anything else you don't want or need, providing it's in good condition. The people in the shop will be very pleased – and you'll be helping someone like Edgar who'll be very grateful indeed.

INTERACTIVE FOLLOW UP ACTIVITIES

Questions
1) Why did Sue Ryder want to help people after the war?
   (There were so many needy people.)
2) What does Sue Ryder Care do?
   (Helps people with disabilities and serious illnesses.)
3) Why does the Sue Ryder charity have shops?
   (To raise money for its work and to run its care centres.)

Getting the message

1) Why do you think people volunteer to help the Sue Ryder Care organisation?
2) Put your hand up when you hear a true statement about volunteers:
   * Volunteers are paid. *(F)*
   * Sue Ryder Care is only run by volunteers. *(F)*
   * Volunteers don't need to have special skills. *(T)*
   * Volunteers give up their time to help others. *(T)*
   * Charity shops run by volunteers raise a lot of money for charities. *(T)*

Learning more

1) Who gives donations to charities like Sue Ryder Care?
2) Are charities the only organisations who help people like Edgar?

NON-INTERACTIVE FOLLOW UP

Summary of the story

* Sue Ryder was a volunteer nurse who helped people in World War II.
* After the war she set up a charity to care for disabled and seriously ill people.
* The charity became known as Sue Ryder Care.
* Sue Ryder Care runs 18 Care Centres that look after needy people like Edgar.
* The organisation depends on raising money and donations.
* Sue Ryder Care has 430 shops run by volunteers who give up their time to help others.
* Sue Ryder was given the title of Lady Ryder; she died in the year 2000.

Something to think about

1) What would happen to Sue Ryder Care if there were no volunteers?
2) How can you help someone like Edgar?

Reflection

Sue Ryder was a kind, hard-working woman who devoted her life to helping others. Remember her, and remember all the volunteers who help people like Edgar. Think how you can help too, perhaps by taking something to a charity shop.

Prayer

Lord God, thank you for Sue Ryder and for the work of all the volunteers and workers who are involved in her charity. Thank you that there are kind people who give up their time to help those people, like Edgar, who can't help themselves as much as they would like to. Help us to remember that we can help too, by taking things to charity shops. Amen.

2i THE RANGE OF IDENTITIES IN THE UK

Objective
To help children appreciate the range of national, regional, religious and ethnic identities in the UK.

PSHE/Citizenship links
2i (Range of identities)

Preparation
This assembly is written in a play script format, and requires four volunteer children to read a part. The ideal presenters would be four good readers from Y5 or Y6 with strong clear voices – any mixture of boys and girls. A short practice before the assembly would be very helpful, and each child will need a copy of the script.

Introduction
Bhavesh is a Year 4 boy who lives in London. He goes to a large primary school in the city, which is near to a very big university. Students and teachers and professors and researchers and all sorts of people from all over the world work at the university, and many of these people have children who go to Bhavesh's school. This makes the school really interesting – let's find out about his class…

PLAY: BHAVESH'S AMAZING CLASS

A   There are 31 children in Class 4Y at Bhavesh's school in London.
B   Most of the children, like Bhavesh, were born in Britain.
C   But some of his classmates come from places thousands of miles away.
D   Bhavesh's friend Karl is from Germany.
A   Juliana is from Holland.
B   Another of Bhavesh's friends is called Gamal – he was born in Egypt.
C   Kim is from South Korea.
D   Paul's mum works at the university – his family is from the USA.
A   Brooke is the oldest girl in the class – she's also American.
B   Ashley and George are twins from Australia.
C   And another of Bhavesh's best friends was brought up in India – he's called Ranjeet.
D   There are also 22 British children in the class, including Bhavesh.
A   But they're not all from London…
B   Laura is from Scotland – she moved to the school two years ago.
C   Hannah's mum is Welsh, so that makes Hannah half Welsh!
D   I wonder which half it is…
A   The remaining 20 members of the class are from England.
B   But only 14 of them are from in and around London.
C   So where are the rest of them from?
D   They're from different regions of the country…
A   Stephen is from Sunderland in the North East.

B Adele is from Walsall – that's in the Midlands.

C Lizzie is from Cheshire in the North West.

D And Scott was born in Devon, which is in the South-West of Britain.

A Mai is new to Bhavesh's school – she comes from Portsmouth on the south coast.

B And Petta is from a village in Norfolk, which is in the east of England.

C So that's where they're all from.

D So what about religions? I bet the children belong to lots of different faiths.

A Yes, there are Christians, Muslims, Jews and Hindus in Bhavesh's class.

B And, of course, there are people who don't follow any religion.

C The Christians belong to different groups too…

D There are Roman Catholics and children who go to the Church of England.

A And one who goes to a Pentecostal church.

B What a lot of different groups there are in one class!

C The children also look quite different from each other.

D Why's that?

A Well, they are from different parts of the world.

B There are people whose families originally come from Asia, like Bhavesh.

C Most of them have dark hair and light brown skin.

D There are also children with much darker skin.

A They are Afro-Caribbean children.

B That's a cool name.

C The children with light skin and hair are mostly Europeans.

D And there are two children from Eastern Asia.

A They have light skin and straight dark hair.

B That's amazing – what a mixture!

C Yeah, and all of them in just one class…

D I wonder if your class is the same?

INTERACTIVE FOLLOW UP ACTIVITIES

Questions

1) Why is there such a mixture of children in Bhavesh's class?

   (Because the school is in London; parents working at the university; Britain contains many different groups of people.)

2) What nationalities are in Bhavesh's class?

   (British, German, Dutch, Egyptian, Korean, Australian, American and Indian.)

3) The children are a mix of different nationalities. How else are they different to each other?

   (Different regions, religions and ethnic groups.)

Getting the message

1) What can we learn about The United Kingdom from this assembly?

   (That it includes a really wide range of different identities.)

2) Here are four statements – give a thumbs up to the ones you agree with and a thumbs down to the ones you don't agree with. If you're in the middle or not sure hold out a flat hand, palm down.
   a. British people have lots of different backgrounds, e.g. different religions.
   b. People in Britain only speak English.
   c. It is not always helpful to put people into categories or groups.
   d. People from other countries who live in Britain sometimes get treated badly.

Learning more

1) Why is it sometimes difficult for children when they move to a new school in a different area or different country?
2) In which countries/regions were you born?
   (Have a show of hands for UK then ask children individually who were born outside the UK.)

NON-INTERACTIVE FOLLOW UP

Summary of the assembly

- Bhavesh goes to a primary school in London.
- There are children from lots of different places at the school.
- Many of the pupils' parents work at the nearby university.
- The British children in the class come from many different regions of the country.
- There are several religions represented in the class.
- The children also belong to different ethnic groups.

Something to think about

1) How can we learn about children from other places?
2) Why is it sometimes difficult to settle when you move to a new school?

Reflection

Britain is made up of a huge variety of people from all sorts of different backgrounds. Life would be very boring and dull if everyone was the same. Try to get to know people who are different from you and find out about their lives.

Prayer

Lord God, thank you that we live in such an interesting world. Please help us to respect and understand people who are different from us. Help to appreciate the great variety of people in the UK. Amen.

2j RESOURCES

Objective
To enable children to appreciate how resources are allocated in different ways and how people are affected by the allocation of resources.

PSHE/Citizenship links
2j (The allocation of resources)

Props
(Not essential): a tool such as a saw, hammer or screwdriver

Introduction
Tools are easy to come by in this country. We have them in school and at home and if we need more they are easy to buy from all sorts of shops. We sometimes borrow them from our neighbours too. Some people never use tools and pay for builders or odd-job workers to bring their own tools when a job needs doing. But how would we manage if we didn't have any tools? How would we fix things and make new things?

A CHARITY IN ACTION – WORKAID

One of the problems for the poorest people of the world is that they have to rely on other people. If there is no rain and their crops don't grow, they often run out of food and have to rely on people to send food from other countries. Or perhaps there is a war in their country and they are forced to leave their homes; then they have to rely on other people to provide them with land and shelter and water.

Relying on others can make poor people feel helpless. Sometimes people live in peace and there may be enough rain for the crops to grow, but they have no tools with which to harvest what is in the fields, or they cannot dig to sow seeds for next year. People also need tools to repair their homes and to make clothes and shoes. But tools are expensive in places like Africa. Poor people simply cannot afford to buy them.

So, in countries like Uganda and Mozambique, many people stay poor and hungry. They cannot grow much food because they lack the tools. They cannot build good houses because they lack the tools. They cannot make things to sell to bring in money for medicines and for clothes because they lack the tools.

But here in the rich countries of the world, like Britain, we have more tools than we need. In many homes there are tools lying around unused, or rusting in a garden shed. Perhaps they belong to a carpenter, who has now retired, or perhaps they were unwanted Christmas presents, or maybe someone has bought a set of shiny new tools and has just left the old ones at the bottom of a cupboard in the garage.

This situation seems very unfair, and a number of charities have been set up to collect unused tools to send to people who really need them.

One of these charities is called Workaid. It is based in Amersham in South East England. Workaid doesn't just send tools to Africa – it collects tools, repairs them, and gives them to all sorts of people who need them, both in the UK and abroad.

Workaid aims to give whole collections of tools to groups who run training projects, so that the people who receive the equipment can also learn how to use it properly.

Workaid gives people the chance to learn practical skills so that they can help themselves and don't have to always rely on other people. The charity collects three groups of tools: firstly, garden tools such as spades, rakes, forks, hoes and pickaxes. Secondly, it collects tools for construction and woodwork, such as hammers, saws, drills, spanners, vices and screwdrivers. And thirdly, it collects tools for making clothes and working with leather, such as sewing machines, knitting machines, tape measures and even pins and needles.

Since 1986 Workaid has supplied needy people with over 100,000 hand tools, 5,000 typewriters and 5,400 sewing machines as well as lots of other useful equipment. So what actually happens to all of these tools?

The volunteers who run Workaid are particularly keen to donate tools to training centres which work with the most disadvantaged people around the world, such as people from poor areas who are orphaned or disabled. A number of the projects that Workaid has supported are in Kenya, a country in Africa.

The Irene Training College for the Blind in Meru, Kenya, has 16 female students. This small school receives no outside help but still manages to teach the girls to use sewing and knitting machines successfully. Some of these machines are provided by Workaid. The students also grow their own vegetables on a small plot of land next to the school. Once again, tools are needed for this, as the college has no money to buy them. The tools that Workaid provides help to give the girls independence – something which is extremely precious.

This is just one of many projects which Workaid helps. The charity receives lots of letters from grateful people, like this one:

'We are absolutely delighted with the tools and equipment you have sent us. They will make such a difference to the work we can do to give practical training to our children who have learning disabilities and multiple handicaps.

Thank you so much.'
From Patti Squire, Head of Mengo & Guluddene Units, Uganda

This letter shows that something like a simple hand tool, which is such an ordinary everyday thing to us, can change the life of someone else.

INTERACTIVE FOLLOW UP ACTIVITIES

Questions

1) What does the charity Workaid do?

   (Collects, repairs and distributes tools to people who need them to become self-reliant.)

2) What do people in places like Kenya need the tools for?

   (For training people, for growing things, for repairing buildings etc, for making things like clothes, and for learning new skills.)

3) Why is giving tools better than giving only food?

   (With tools, people can grow their own food – they can become independent.)

Getting the message

1) What does today's assembly teach us about how available tools are in different countries of the world?

    (People in wealthier countries have more choice; they can also use what they buy e.g. tools, to earn more money and goods.)

2) Give these statements a score using your fingers: no fingers if it's not a good idea, five if it's quite a good idea and ten if you think it's a very good idea.

    • More people should support charities like Workaid.

    • It would be better just to give poor people money.

    • The governments of wealthy countries like the UK should send huge amounts of tools to less developed countries.

    • We should help needy people in this country rather than people in other countries.

    • Lottery money should be given to voluntary groups like Workaid.

Learning more

1) Tools are not equally available throughout the world. What else is not shared out evenly?

2) How can you help a charity like Workaid?

NON-INTERACTIVE FOLLOW UP

Summary of the story

• Workaid is a charity, which gives tools to needy people at home and abroad.

• The tools help people who are stuck in poverty to become self-reliant.

• Workaid supports training organisations that teach people new skills, such as using a sewing machine.

• Tools are sent to groups of disadvantaged people, such as disabled children and orphans.

• People use the tools to help them grow food, repair their homes and make things to sell.

• Some people learn a skill and get a job as a result.

Something to think about

1) Why are tools so important?

2) Is it best just to give poor people food and money?

3) Why is there such a difference between the rich and poor nations of the world?

Reflection

Giving someone a tool like a spade can give that person independence. It can allow a person to do something useful – to grow food, to help others, to feel good about himself or herself. If you have lots of something, think how you can share with someone who has little.

Prayer

Lord God, thank you for the kind volunteers at Workaid who give their time to help other people help themselves. Please help Workaid to collect lots of tools and to give them to those most in need. Help the world to become a fairer place. Amen.

Workaid can be contacted via the charity's website: www.home.btclick.com/workaid

2K HOW THE MEDIA PRESENT INFORMATION

Objective
To help children think about the ways in which the media present information about an event.

PSHE/Citizenship links
2k (How the media present information)

Preparation
This assembly is in the form of a short play script or sketch, and requires four volunteer children to read a part. The ideal actors would be four good readers from Y5 or Y6 with strong clear voices – any mixture of boys and girls. A short practice before the assembly would be very helpful, and each child will need a copy of the script.

Introduction
Imagine that the England football manager has been sacked. How would we find out about it?

PLAY: THE MEDIA

A Hey, did you know the England manager's got the sack?

B Yes, I heard about it on the radio in the car this morning.

C I saw it on the TV news at breakfast.

D It was in the newspapers too.

A I read about it on the BBC Sport website last night.

B Yep, it's the big story in the media today.

C Err, what is 'the media'? – I've heard the word, but never understood it.

D The media is all the things we've just mentioned...

A TV, radio, newspapers, websites and there are magazines too.

B They're all the ways we find out the latest information and news.

C Oh right, I see.

D I wonder if all the different types of media present the story in the same way.

A I doubt it.

B The tabloid newspapers were pleased to see the England manager go – one headline I saw said 'Good Riddance!'

C My dad said that his newspaper reckoned it was the wrong decision. They said that the England team were struggling because of injuries, not because of the manager.

D There wasn't much about it on the radio – just a few seconds on the news.

A Well, there was loads about it on the TV news this morning. They were talking about the reasons he lost the job and interviewing footballers about who might be the next manager.

B The local radio station were talking about it too because there's a rumour that the next England manager might be from one of the local clubs.

C You get local TV and local newspapers too – I expect they'll be covering that story.

D What about football magazines though? They only come out every week or every month.

A They'll probably be doing lots of research about the story, and interviewing other managers for opinions, and looking at stats and stuff.

B What for?

C So they can write long detailed articles about it. They can't include up to date news, but they've got more time to put together their information.

D What I can't understand is the tabloid newspapers – they always go mad about things like this

A You mean they're always saying controversial things?

B Yes – they do that to grab people's attention so they can sell more papers.

C But the BBC news don't report like that.

D That's because the BBC is an independent organisation.

A What does that mean?

B It isn't owned by anyone who can tell the editors and reporters what to say.

C Does that happen with newspapers?

D Yes, with some of them – the owner likes them to support certain things like a particular political party.

A So the BBC is not allowed to take sides you mean?

B That's right.

C Most radio stations are the same too – they have to present the news fairly.

D And they have to check their facts carefully too.

A Yes, if they get things wrong people can take them to court.

B Oh yes – that happens with gossip magazines who take photos of celebrities without their permission.

C You don't read those do you?

D Err, no – I've just seen them at the hairdresser's…

A So anyway, I wonder how the media will be following up the England footy story?

B Well, the tabloid newspapers will be suggesting who they think should be the next manager.

C And so will the broadsheet newspapers.

D Hang on, which are the tabloids and which are the broadsheet newspapers?

A The tabloids are smaller papers.

B Like the *Sun*, the *Mirror* and the *Daily Mail*.

C The broadsheets are the bigger ones like *The Times*, the *Telegraph* and the *Guardian*.

D I thought they're called the 'quality' newspapers.

A They are – it's just another name for them.

B So all the media – papers, TV, and radio and so on present news and information in different ways?

C Yes, the good thing is that we have a choice.

Interactive Follow Up Activities

Questions

1) What is 'the media'?

   (TV, newspapers, radio, magazines, websites.)

2) Do all the media report news and information in the same way?

   (No, newspapers and magazines often give opinions, but TV and radio newsreaders report facts and information, although reporters often interview people with strong opinions.)

3) The BBC is an independent organisation – what does independent mean?

   (It means it is not owned or controlled by a person, a company or the government.)

Getting the message

1) Should we always believe what we read?

   (Not always – newspapers and magazines do make mistakes and include opinions not just facts. The TV news is more reliable.)

2) Who works for the media? Give these people a thumbs up if they do, and a thumbs down if they don't.

   - Journalists ✓
   - Poets *(very occasionally)*
   - Newsreaders ✓
   - Reporters ✓
   - Photographers *(some do)*
   - Newspaper editors ✓
   - Farmers

Learning more

1) Why is it good to have lots of different types of media?

   (So we can choose; so we can keep up with news and information; so the needs and preferences of different audiences / consumers can be met.)

2) Why do some people not like or trust the media?

   (The media publicise crime; they can give people a bad name sometimes by criticising them in public, e.g. politicians; they also sometimes publish things that people would prefer to keep private.)

NON-INTERACTIVE FOLLOW UP

Summary of the play

- The media is the collective name for TV, radio and newspapers, plus magazines and parts of the internet.
- The media report news and pass on information and opinions to the public.
- Newspapers are owned by people or companies and can write opinions and news.
- The BBC is an independent organisation and must report the news without any bias.

Something to think about

1) Why is the media important?
2) Should we listen to the news or doesn't it matter?

Reflection

Try to listen to the news and read about what is going on in the world. Ask questions about what's going on and think about events. It is good that we have so many different choices in the media, so make the most of them.

Prayer

Lord God, thank you that we have the media to keep us aware of what is going on in the world. Help us to understand the news and to keep ourselves informed. Amen.

3A Healthy Living: Exercise

Objective
To help children understand the benefits of exercise.

PSHE/Citizenship links
3a (Healthy lifestyle/benefits of exercise), 5a (taking responsibility)

Props
(Not essential): a digital watch and a pair of swimming goggles

Introduction
I wonder what it's like being in a TV series? Today's story is about a boy who had a chance to be on TV, and then was helped by these (hold up watch and goggles).

Story: Swimming the Hill

The day had started with such excitement. Joel, along with eleven of his friends from primary school, had been chosen to audition for an episode of a new TV series. The programme was going to be called 'Felicity's Farm', and was set in the Yorkshire Dales. The story was about a group of schoolchildren who visit the farm and go mad, causing all sorts of chaos. The TV producers had arranged transport, costumes, a delicious lunch and were even going to pay the children who were chosen to be extras.

But the day had passed, and now Joel was in tears. He was sitting in the kitchen at home with his dad.

"Nearly all my friends got chosen – it's not fair.'"

"I'm really sorry Joel," said Dad, putting a comforting hand on his shoulder.

"They're all gonna be on telly – and they'll get £50 each…"

"So tell me what happened." Dad pulled up a chair next to Joel's.

"Well, the morning was OK – we put on the clothes they gave us and they filmed us getting off this bus. There was a lot of hanging around too."

"And what did you do in the afternoon?"

"Well, that's when we had to run up a hill pretending to chase some sheep."

"Sounds like fun to me."

"It wasn't fun Dad – it was awful – the hill was massive, I couldn't breathe and… and I didn't keep up with the others."

"What happened then?"

"This woman from the TV people told me to go and sit down and get a drink, then about an hour later they got us all together and they read out a list of names." Joel began to sob again; Dad gave him a hug.

"Hey, never mind – I still think you're the best."

Later that evening Joel wandered into the kitchen where Dad was washing up.

"I know what the trouble is Dad – I'm not fit."

"Well, Joel, I think maybe you're right there."

"But I eat well though, don't I? I eat loads more salad and vegetables than most of my friends."

"That's true: you're really good with food, but you don't get much exercise. To be healthy you need a good diet *and* exercise. Why don't you go to football coaching after school?"

"Dad, you know I hate football."

"Well, what about bike riding? I could go out with you."

"That's kind of OK, but I still get nervous in traffic."

"Tennis?"

"I like tennis, but I'm just not very good at hitting the ball – remember those kids on the summer course laughed at me last year."

"So, what are you going to do Joel?"

"The only thing I really like is swimming but everyone messes around in the pool on Saturdays – it's just too overcrowded."

"Well I like swimming too – how about getting up early on Friday and we'll go down to the quiet session and do some lengths?"

"Just swimming lengths sounds boring."

"You're just scared because I can beat you…"

"Dad! Come on, you're joking."

"Right, we'll see: seven forty-five a.m. on Friday."

"Seven forty-five!"

Joel dived into the warm water, which finally woke him up properly. Getting up half an hour early was a lot harder than it sounded.

"Come on Dad – let's have a race then!"

"Hey, hang on; you're supposed to warm up. Let's do five lengths each first." After the warm up they raced a single length of the pool, with Dad narrowly winning.

"That was fun," said Joel. "I reckon I'll beat you soon though."

"I'm sure you will – but come on now, let's do ten lengths each." After this, they stopped for a rest.

"I was right Dad, just going up and down is boring."

"Here you are – this'll make it more interesting." Dad unfastened the watch off his wrist; Joel hadn't noticed that it was new. "I bought this for you – so you can time yourself."

Joel's eyes widened. "Oh cool – a Nixon Number 8 – thanks Dad!" He fixed the sleek blue watch onto his wrist. "What's your best time for swimming ten lengths then Dad?"

"Oh, I can do it in… four minutes sixteen seconds."

"Right; I'm going to beat that." Joel launched himself off the side of the pool and went splashing away with front crawl to swim another ten lengths. Dad smiled as he watched his son go. Joel was breathless and a little disappointed at the end when the watch's digital display said 5 minutes 3 seconds.

"Don't worry – you'll improve," said Dad.

Over the next few weeks Joel and Dad went to the pool twice a week before school. Joel was determined to beat Dad's time. His second try was 4.56 and after that he managed 4.48. The more he practised, the quicker he became. He did 4.47, 4.30, 4.22, and after five weeks it happened. Joel touched the side after ten rocket powered lengths and hit the stopwatch button: 4.13! He'd done it.

Dad was just as pleased as Joel.

"That's fantastic – now all we need is a TV series about a group of kids who go mad in a swimming pool…"

INTERACTIVE FOLLOW UP ACTIVITIES

Questions

1) Why didn't Joel get chosen to be in the TV series?

   (He couldn't run up a hill.)

2) Did swimming make Joel fit and healthy very quickly?

   (No – it takes weeks or months of regular exercise to become fit.)

3) Why did Joel's dad offer to go riding and swimming with him, instead of suggesting he should go with his friends?

   (To encourage Joel, and to save him embarrassment.)

Getting the message

1) What was the main message of this story?

   (That exercise is important; lots of different types of exercise are good; you feel good when you're fit.)

2) Here are four messages: vote for the ones you agree with by putting up your hand:

   • Exercise helps you get on TV.

   • Exercise is important.

   • Swimming is the best kind of exercise.

   • You feel good when you're fit.

Learning more

1) Mini quiz: ask for 3 volunteers to come out and answer true or false to these questions:

   • Only children need to exercise regularly. *(F)*

   • A lot of adults have heart problems because they don't exercise enough. *(T)*

   • Occasional exercise is just as good as regular exercise. *(F)*

2) Name some sports or activities that are good exercise.

3) For each of these activities, call out 'yes' if it's good exercise, and 'no' if it isn't (no shouting):

   • gymnastics

   • basketball

   • snooker

   • PlayStation

   • jogging

4) Give each of these activities a score by showing fingers, as follows: 1 finger = little exercise; 5 fingers = quite good exercise; 10 fingers = excellent exercise.

   • walking the dog

   • trampolining

   • mountain biking

   • dancing

   • playing card games

   • ten-pin bowling

NON-INTERACTIVE FOLLOW UP

Summary of the story
- Joel missed his chance to be on TV because he wasn't fit enough to run up a hill.
- His dad encouraged him to do a sport he enjoyed: swimming.
- Joel practised and set himself a target to beat.
- He improved at swimming, and became fitter and more healthy; he felt better too.

Something to think about
1) Do you get regular exercise?
2) Do you do sports, or just play lots of computer games and watch TV?
3) Exercise can help you feel good, have fun and stop you getting serious illnesses when you grow up.

Reflection
Look after your heart – it's the only one you've got. Think how you can be active: do some exercise that you enjoy and do it regularly. Join a club or go with friends.

Prayer
Lord God, thank you that there are lots of ways to exercise and that many of them are fun. Help me to be active and to stay healthy. Amen.

© Badger Publishing Ltd.

3A (2) HEALTHY EATING

Objective
To help children understand the benefits of a healthy diet.

PSHE/Citizenship links
3a (Healthy eating)

Props
(Not essential): an apple

Introduction
Food is very important – we couldn't live without it. But food can help to keep us healthy or it can actually harm us. Listen to this unlikely story and you'll see what I mean.

STORY: THE HUNGRY ALIEN

An alien crash-landed on Earth one day. He was flying from Delta Centuri to visit some relations on Neptune when he ran out of fuel. Although it came down with a mighty bump, his flying saucer actually landed on top of a bubblewrap warehouse and so the alien was unhurt. The warehouse was completely wrecked, but we won't worry about that.

The alien was hungry, so he decided to look for some food. He saw a man mowing the lawn in his back garden.

"Hello man," he said (oh, I forgot to tell you – the alien spoke excellent English).

"Hello – can I help you?" said the man.

"Yes, I hope so," said the alien. "I've crash landed on your planet and I'm very hungry – do you have anything I can eat?"

"Yes, of course – if you just hang on for ten minutes while I finish this job, I'll get you a sandwich."

"That's very kind," said the alien. "But I don't think I can wait for ten minutes."

"Oh, why's that then?"

"Well, where I come from – Delta Centuri – everyone has to eat something at least every five minutes. We have very fast metabolisms you see – that means we use up energy very quickly. Our hearts beat 788 times a minute, and we only live for one year. So, I must eat very soon, you see."

"Ah," said the man. "I see... and it's a bit of a problem because I promised my wife that I'd finish the lawn before 'The Antiques Roadshow' was on... but I tell you what – I've had a good idea. If you go into the house, through that door there, you'll find my daughter Melody in the kitchen. She's only seven years old, but I'm sure she'll be able to fix you up with something nice to eat." And with that he carried on mowing the lawn.

In the kitchen, the alien saw a girl wearing green jeans and an Aston Villa shirt.

"Hello Melody," he said.

"Hello – you look like an alien," said Melody.

"Yes, I am – a hungry alien."

"Oh, shall I get you something to eat?"

"Yes please."

A minute later, just in time, the alien was tucking into a squelchy cream doughnut.

"This is delicious Melody – is this what Earth people eat all the time?"

"No, we eat lots of things – look I'll show you." Melody went over to the giant refrigerator in the corner and opened the door. It was crammed with the week's shopping.

"Oh wow!" said the alien. "This is good news for me because I have to eat every five minutes or I pass out."

"In that case," said Melody, "I will take care of you – I'll make sure you're fed and that you get to try a big range of Earth foods. How does that sound?"

"It sounds just the ticket," said the alien. "But won't the rest of your family mind?"

"Oh no – they're too busy watching 'The Antiques Roadshow'."

Two hours later, the alien and Melody were still in the kitchen. There were empty packets, tins, boxes, wrappers and foil dishes everywhere. He had tried cakes, sausages, chips, cheese toasties, sweets, chicken nuggets, ice cream, burgers, chocolate, microwave puddings, pizzas, pastries and pies. The fridge was nearly empty and Melody was exhausted. The alien had been to the loo an extraordinary number of times.

"This Earth food is really delicious," he said. "And it's very convenient – so quick to prepare."

"You're not still hungry though are you?" said Melody wearily.

"Well, I will be in four minutes or so, but I'll stop for a little lie down first – I am feeling a bit strange."

While the alien was resting, Melody went through the cupboards in the kitchen searching for more food. She also rang her best friend Coral to ask if she could bring some food round.

A week later, the alien was still in Melody's kitchen. So were twelve other boys and girls who were Melody's friends. They were all working together to feed the hungry alien. By this time, the alien had tried much more – tinned beef curry and packet soups, Frosties, toffee, fried eggs, bacon, Pop Tarts, pancakes with syrup, crisps, Yorkshire puddings, hot dogs, biscuits and jam roly poly.

But he was beginning to look peculiar. His skin was slightly grey and he kept having to lie down – he had definitely put on weight. Also, he was no longer chatty like before – he just sat and ate quietly, hardly even turning to say thank you when the meals were brought to him.

Three weeks later, the alien looked even worse. He just lay on the kitchen floor half asleep while the children carefully pushed pieces of caramel and poppadom into his mouth.

"He looks terrible," said Melody. "What shall we do?"

"My mum's a nurse," said Coral. "I'll ask her to come and have a look at him."
She did.

Coral's mum bent over the alien's bloated body and listened to his breathing. Then she felt his pulse. The girls explained that he needed to eat every five minutes because his metabolism was very fast.

"I see," she said. "So, what have you been feeding him?" They told her.

"Well, no wonder he's ill!" said Coral's mum with wide eyes. "You've given him a shocking diet."

"What do mean?" said Melody. "He's definitely not on a diet."

"No – your diet just means all the things you eat. You've given him far too much fat and sugar and salt. His heart is in a terrible state."

"Oh, we're sorry," said Coral. "It was just quicker to get packets and tins and things like that."'

"A bit of convenience food is OK," said Coral's mum, "but aliens are the same as us – they need a balance of different kinds of foods."

"What do you mean?" said Melanie.

"Well, he needs fresh fruit and vegetables for a start, for fibre and vitamins. Then he needs energy foods like pasta and bread and rice and cereals. And he needs body-building foods like fish and eggs and meat."

"But there's meat in sausages, and he has had some cereals, like Cocoa Flakes."

"You're right, but those have lots of fat and sugar and additives too. He's just had far too much of that and little bits of fat have blocked his blood vessels. It's a good job you called me."

Coral's mum made the alien a brown bread tuna sandwich with salad, and a yoghurt. She gave him plenty of water too, instead of all the sugary fizz that he'd been drinking. After a few more weeks of healthy food, with a good balance, the alien began to recover.

A team of scientists and engineers repaired his flying saucer and soon he was ready to fly home. He was even forgiven for wrecking the bubblewrap warehouse. He thanked Melody and her friends for their kindness and told them he would visit again sometime, but before zooming away he wrote a Post-it note and put it on his control panel. It said: *If visiting Earth, be very careful what you eat.*

INTERACTIVE FOLLOW UP ACTIVITIES

Questions

1) Why did the alien get poorly?
   (He had eaten too much sugary, fatty food.)
2) Why did Melody and her friends give the alien unhealthy food?
   (It was convenient or easy; it saved time; it was the type of food that they enjoyed most themselves.)
3) What types of food was the alien not getting?
   (E.g. fresh fruit and veg, bread, white meat, etc.)

Getting the message

1) This story is not very realistic, but we can still learn something from it. What can we learn from this story?
   (That we need to eat a balanced diet to keep healthy.)
2) True or false? (Each time ask for a show of hands for true and a show of hands for false.)
   • It's ok to eat fatty foods as long as you don't eat them too often. *(T)*
   • People who say "I don't like vegetables" probably have a balanced diet. *(F)*
   • Packets and tins don't tell you how much fat and salt they contain. *(F)*
   • Baked beans, ketchup and take-aways usually contain lots of salt and sugar. *(T)*
   • Many children who eat a lot of junk food become overweight. *(T)*

Learning more

1) Many puddings contain lots of added sugar – are there any which do not?

   (E.g. fruit, plain yoghurts, nuts.)

2) What problems can an unhealthy diet lead to in later life?

   (Weight problems, heart disease, skin problems, poor teeth and bones, lack of resistance to disease, etc.)

NON-INTERACTIVE FOLLOW UP

Summary of the story

- A alien crash lands on Earth.
- He needs to eat every five minutes because of his high metabolism.
- A girl called Melody and her friends feed the alien.
- They give him lots of high-fat, high-sugar and salty food from packets and tins.
- He begins to feel unwell with heart problems and is rescued by Coral's mum, a nurse.
- She gives him healthy food and he recovers before flying home.

Something to think about

1) Why is eating a healthy diet important for everyone?
2) What is a balanced diet?
3) What can I do if I love sweets and chocolates and fried food, but hate vegetables?

Reflection

We only have one body, which must last us for a lifetime. We need to give our body special fuel called food. If we give our bodies too much junk then they will stop working properly and we will not feel well. We need to eat a balance of different foods, with plenty of fresh fruit, vegetables and bread particularly.

Prayer

Lord God, please help us to look after our bodies by eating a healthy balanced diet. Help us to resist the temptation to eat too many sweets and too much fatty junk food. Help us to remember how important fresh vegetables and fruit are, and thank you for making so many lovely natural things that we can eat. Amen.

3B THE DANGERS OF BACTERIA

Objective

To help children understand that bacteria and viruses can affect health and that following simple, safe routines can reduce their spread.

PSHE/Citizenship links

3b (Bacteria and viruses)

Props

(Not essential): a dishcloth, a chopping board, a large knife (or possibly a simple drawing of one on a piece of card!)

Introduction

Have you ever looked forward to something that should have been a real treat, but that turned out to be a major disaster? Danny had an experience like that last year. Listen carefully to the story, and see if you can pick up the clues to what goes wrong and who is the cause of all the bother.

STORY: WHAT'S BUGGING YOU?

Danny, his brother Sam and their cousin Lizzie were bouncing on the huge trampoline that was in the garden. Danny had longed for a trampoline... well, practically FOREVER and today, on his tenth birthday, his wish had finally come true. For his party he'd asked for a big barbeque with his family in their garden. Danny's Dad and Uncle Ray were busy setting out the patio furniture and lighting the barbeque outside. They'd already put up loads of balloons all round the garden and laid the picnic table with special birthday plates, paper cups and the knives and forks. There was a table crammed with bottles of coke and lemonade to drink, ketchup and mustard to squirt on the food, and crisps to nibble on while they waited for the barbeque to be ready. This was going to be a birthday he'd never forget, he was sure of it!

Mum and Auntie Sadie were in the kitchen, preparing the food.

"What've we got on the menu today then, Pam?" asked Auntie Sadie.

"Well, I've got some nice salads already made – they're in the fridge to keep them cool; there'll be some French bread, piles of sausages and I've got some gorgeous bits of chicken to make kebabs with. I thought we could cut it up into chunks and put them onto skewers with some pieces of onion or some peppers."

"Fantastic!" said Auntie Sadie enthusiastically, "What can I do to help?"

"Right, well, if I give you the chicken, the onions and the peppers, can you cut them all up and thread them onto these skewers, while I get on with the fruit salad over here?" answered Mum. "Here's a chopping board to cut the raw chicken up on, and a knife – it's a nice new one, the sharpest one I've got, so you'll be finished in no time!"

"Okay – let me at it!" laughed Auntie Sadie as she put on an apron. "I'll just wash my hands before I start."

Meanwhile, outside, the Dads seemed to have finished their work and were busy 'testing' the new patio chairs and making sure that the beer tasted okay...

Mum and Auntie Sadie chatted happily as they worked on the kebabs and the fruit salad. They talked about their children and how fast they seemed to be growing up. "I can't believe that Danny has reached double figures already – I just don't know where the time has gone!" sighed Mum, with a bit of a tear in her eye. "How are you doing with those kebabs, Sadie?"

"I've nearly finished," came the reply. "You were right, you know: that new knife of yours cuts like a dream!"

"That's good, because I'm really struggling with this one here," laughed Mum. "Tell you what – you can help me cut up this fruit when you've made the kebabs."

"Okay – I'm on the last one now," said Auntie Sadie. "There we are – all done!"

"Oh, they look fantastic, Sadie. Ray! Bob! Come and get the kebabs and the sausages: they can go onto the barbeque now."

Uncle Ray heaved himself reluctantly out of his seat, but cheered up when he saw the delicious looking kebabs. "Now mind you cook them right the way through, Ray," said Mum. "I don't want anyone being ill from undercooked meat!"

Auntie Sadie gave her chopping board a quick wipe with a dishcloth and got straight on with chopping up a pile of apples and pears with Mum's new knife. By the time the fruit salad was finished, there was a delicious smell of barbequing chicken wafting in from outside. In the garden, Dad and Uncle Ray were standing over the barbeque, poking the coals, turning the kebabs and pretending to be on 'Ready Steady Cook'. The children were hot and sweaty and having a rest from bouncing. They were happily sipping cool lemonade and pretending to be part of the audience. Uncle Ray was on top form and soon had them in stitches. Danny laughed so much at one of his corny jokes, that the lemonade he was drinking squirted down his nose and made him choke!

"Oh, Ray!" moaned Auntie Sadie, coming out to see what the noise was all about. "You're just not concentrating, are you? You've knocked half of the cutlery onto the floor with your clowning about! Hand it over and I'll give it a wipe with my dishcloth: we can't eat using mucky knives and forks!"

Eventually things calmed down a bit, the meat was fully cooked, and the rest of the food was brought out. Everyone tucked in, and they all agreed that it was one of the best birthday parties that they'd ever had.

A couple of days later Danny was sent home from school. He'd been really sick – all over the floor in the classroom – and he felt terrible. He hated getting tummy bugs! He was amazed to find his brother Sam already tucked up in bed when his Mum brought him home: he must have caught the same bug at school. Things went from bad to worse, though, because Mum went down with exactly the same and that night they had a phone call from Auntie Sadie to say that poor Lizzie had been sick at school, and now Uncle Ray wasn't feeling too hot either.

In the end everyone who'd been at the party was ill, and they were so poorly that they had to call the doctor. He said, "I'm afraid that this looks like a nasty case of food poisoning. Have you all eaten any undercooked meat recently – maybe at a barbeque?"

"No, it can't have been the meat," groaned Mum. "We made doubly sure that the meat was well cooked, because we know how dangerous it can be if it isn't!"

"Well something has caused you all to be so ill," said the doctor. "You'd better do some detective work to find out what went wrong, or it could easily happen again!"

"Ohh…" groaned Danny, "I couldn't face this again! I knew I was going to have a birthday that I'd never forget, but this isn't quite what I had in mind!"

INTERACTIVE FOLLOW UP ACTIVITIES

Questions

1) Hands up who thinks they know why Danny's family got food poisoning?
   (Don't ask for answers yet.)

2) Who thinks that it was Dad and Uncle Ray's fault because they didn't cook the meat properly? *(Not true.)*

3) Why isn't that right? *(Because in the story it says that 'the meat was fully cooked'.)*

4) *(Ask for 3 volunteers to come and hold the props as you mention them.)* Here are some clues to help you decide what went wrong *(give out knife, chopping board and dishcloth).*

5) How do you think that each of these things could have been the cause of the illness?
   - Knife *(Auntie Sadie used the same knife to do the fruit salad that she'd used to cut up the raw chicken, without washing it thoroughly first).*
   - Chopping board *(Auntie Sadie used the same chopping board to cut up the fruit as she'd used for the raw chicken).*
   - Dishcloth *(Auntie Sadie had wiped the chopping board after chopping the chicken, and had then wiped the cutlery that had fallen onto the floor with the same dishcloth).*

6) So who was the 'baddie' in this story? *(Poor old Auntie Sadie.)*

Getting the message

1) Many foods, like raw meat, have dangerous bacteria lurking in them. Cooking the food properly can kill most of these.

2) Here are five things you might do while you are preparing food. Some of them are dangerous. Vote for the ones you think might cause food poisoning:
   - Forget to wash your hands before and after you handle any type of food. ✓
   - Use the same knife to cut up raw meat and other foods. ✓
   - Imagine you are on 'Ready Steady Cook'. ✗
   - Put raw meat near other food you will eat without cooking it first. ✓
   - Use a dishcloth to wipe up raw meat juices, and then use it for something else. ✓

Learning more

1) Mini quiz: ask for 3 volunteers to come out and answer true or false to these questions:
   a. Washing your hands before and after touching food is the most important way to avoid food poisoning. *(T)*
   b. Leaving food uncovered is dangerous: flies can land on it and spread disease. *(T)*
   c. Once food has been cooked, it's okay to leave it out. It doesn't need to be put in a fridge again if you want to keep it. *(F)*

2) Washing your hands is very important. When should you ALWAYS wash your hands?
   (After going to the loo, before eating, before and after preparing food.)

3) What should Auntie Sadie have done when she was preparing the food?
   - ***Thoroughly*** *washed the knife after using it for the chicken, ideally sterilizing it with boiling water, too.*
   - *Thoroughly washed her hands after preparing the chicken (she did wash them beforehand).*
   - *Rinsed the chopping board with boiling water, to kill most of the bacteria on it, and NOT wiped it down with a dishcloth.*
   - *Used a completely different chopping board for the fruit salad.*
   - *Washed the cutlery that fell on the floor properly, and not wiped it with a mucky dishcloth.*

NON-INTERACTIVE FOLLOW UP

Summary of the story
- It was Danny's birthday, so he had a barbeque.
- Mum and Auntie Sadie prepared the food.
- Auntie Sadie used the same knife and chopping board to prepare the fruit salad that she used to cut up raw chicken.
- She forgot to wash her hands after preparing the chicken.
- She also wiped the chopping board with a dishcloth, which she then used to wipe some cutlery.
- Everyone who was at the barbeque became really ill with food poisoning.

Something to think about
1) Think how you can help to avoid spreading bacteria that cause food poisoning, even if you don't do the cooking at your house.
2) Often you just get an upset tummy, but it is possible to become very seriously ill with food poisoning.
3) Usually food is good fun and delicious and there isn't a problem, AS LONG AS you follow simple rules to keep it safe.

Reflection
Watch what you eat and think carefully that you don't do anything that might cause you to become ill.

Prayer
Lord God, thank you that there are so many good things for us to enjoy eating. Help us to be sensible in the ways we prepare and keep our food, so that it does us good, instead of making us ill. Amen.

3D SUBSTANCES AND DRUGS

Objective

To help children understand the effects and risks of alcohol.

PSHE/Citizenship links

3d (Substances and drugs)

Props

(Not essential): a lager can (empty or full), or other alcoholic drinks container

Introduction

Most adults like to drink alcohol now and again. Some people go to a bar or a pub or have a drink when they are having a meal in a restaurant. Others like to sit at home and have a can of beer or a bottle of wine. A lot of teenagers like to drink alcohol too, and think that getting drunk is funny and cool. But drinking alcohol carries a number of risks, especially for young people, as one boy discovered.

STORY: FRIDAY NIGHT

Friday was a special day in ten year-old Kasan's house – his family were celebrating his older sister winning a big cycling race. He had enjoyed a delicious Indian takeaway for a treat and had just stayed up late to watch a DVD with two of his friends, Michael and Anwar.

"Well, it's half-past ten – I'd better drive these two boys home," said Kasan's father. "We may as well drop off this DVD at the rental shop too."

"Can I come with you Dad?"

"Of course you can, go and get your coat then."

Ten minutes later, Kasan was in the car with his father. They had dropped off Michael and Anwar and were heading into the centre of town to the video shop. It was quite exciting for Kasan – he hardly ever went into town after dark. He was surprised by how many shops and restaurants and bars were open and by how many people were on the streets. There were bright lights everywhere and lots of cars too. Kasan's father couldn't stop near the video shop and so they had to park outside the library further down the street.

"Come on," said Kasan's father as he stepped out of the car. "Let's be as quick as we can." Kasan kept close to his father who was walking at a brisk pace towards the shop. There were lots of people on the pavements, mainly groups of young people. Kasan was amazed at how noisy they were – most of them seemed to be shouting. Kasan's father reached for his hand.

They passed a pub just as three huge men spilt out of the doorway. One of them bumped into Kasan's father and swore at him. Kasan was scared. Why was everyone so loud and rude?

"I'm sorry Kasan," said Dad. "I shouldn't have brought you into town at this time." They reached the shop and dropped off the DVD. Kasan's father suggested that they cross the road before going back to the car. There seemed to be even more people than ever on the streets and quite a few of them were walking on the road. A taxi pulled out of a side street and slammed on its brakes with a screech. The driver had just missed hitting a young man who was crossing the road. His friends were laughing and singing. Kasan was shocked.

A police van came past and stopped. A man stepped out and picked up two traffic cones, which had been thrown into the middle of the road. The group of singing boys shouted towards the van, then went into a pub.

Kasan couldn't believe how rowdy the town was. It was so quiet and nice to go shopping here on Saturdays. Why was it like this on Friday nights? Kasan could now see the car and was relieved to be nearly off the streets. But before they reached it, he felt his father's hand tighten around his and pull him to the edge of the pavement, away from a dark doorway. Kasan looked. There was a girl bent over in the doorway being sick. It was a horrible sight, but what shocked Kasan most was that the girl looked about the same age as his sister, who was just 14.

Kasan's father drove home quickly through the dark streets.

"Were all those people drunk dad?"

"No, but they'd all been drinking and most of them had had too much. It was not a pretty sight was it?"

"It was awful. Why do they do it?"

"That's a good question, Kasan – but let's talk about it tomorrow – it's very late and I want you to go straight to bed."

The following morning, Kasan was up early. He hadn't slept very well – he was too busy thinking about everything he had seen on the streets the night before. He wanted to know more about alcohol and drinking. He decided to ask his mum – she was a doctor and would know all about it for sure. Kasan wandered into the kitchen to get a drink and was pleased to see that his mum was already up.

"Morning dear," she said.

"Mum, alcohol's a drug isn't it?"

"Ah, your father warned me last night that you'd be asking questions about that.' She poured a glass of orange juice for Kasan and sat down. 'The answer is yes – alcohol is a drug, but it's a legal one. What else do you want to know?"

"Those people we saw last night were acting so stupid – was that the alcohol then?"

"It most probably was, yes," said Kasan's mum. "Like all other drugs, alcohol affects the way our brain and our body works."

"What does it do then?"

"Well, alcohol is what we call a depressant. It slows down the working of the brain."

"But how does it reach your brain?"

"Drugs are absorbed into the blood stream you see, and they travel all round the body. Alcohol even gets into your hair."

"So why were the people on the streets being rowdy and clumsy?"

"If you abuse alcohol and drink too much then it can do all sorts of things to you – it makes some people loud and aggressive, but it also affects your co-ordination and slows down your reaction times."

"Is that why people are not allowed to drive cars after they've been drinking?"

"Exactly right – you're much more likely to have an accident."

"We saw a man nearly get run over, Mum."

"I'm not surprised, Kasan, people lose their sense of judgement when they have too much alcohol in their bloodstream."

"But Mum, if you know it's so bad for you, why do you and Dad both drink it?"

Kasan's mum chuckled. "I knew you were going to ask that, and it's a good question. We only drink a small amount of alcohol – usually just two or three glasses of wine at the weekend, for instance, and that's fine. It's only drinking too much alcohol that causes problems."

"So why do teenagers and people in their twenties drink so much?"

"That's another good question Kasan. They think it's cool and they do it because their friends do it – and because it does make them feel good at first."

"But that girl who was being sick wasn't feeling good."

"No, the problem is that a lot of young people don't know when to stop. Alcohol is also addictive, and some people, called alcoholics, are hooked on it."

"What happens to them?"

"Well, I see quite a few of them in my surgery and it's very sad. For a start, alcohol can damage the brain, the stomach, the heart and the liver especially. Many of them get very ill from it. But it also damages their lives and their families – sometimes just the cost of drinking can cause people to get into terrible debt."

"How much does it cost?"

"Well if you are a moderate drinker and have, say, 4 pints of beer, two glasses of wine and a gin and tonic a week, then after 5 years you will have spent about £3800."

"What! How did you work that out Mum?"

"Well, as a doctor, I get lots of leaflets with facts and figures sent to me. And one of them also points out that a person who drinks 12 pints of beer a week will have spent about £6500 after 5 years – you could buy a car with that. Oh look at the time – I have to go now love – bye."

Kasan watched his mum go out of the door. He soon forgot the facts and figures she told him, but he never did forget his Friday night trip to the video shop.

INTERACTIVE FOLLOW UP ACTIVITIES

Questions

1) Why was the town so busy that night?
   (A lot of people go out on Friday night because it's the start of the weekend.)
2) What were the young people on the streets doing?
   (Being rowdy, pushing, shouting, walking on the road, throwing traffic cones and being sick.)
3) Why do young people drink so much alcohol if it can be a dangerous drug?
   (They enjoy it, think it's cool, peer pressure, it makes people feel better, etc.)

Getting the message

1) What did we find out about alcohol from this story?

   (It affects the brain and slows down reactions; it affects co-ordination; it can make some people aggressive; drinking too much can damage parts of the body such as the liver; it is addictive; it alters a person's mood.)

2) What are the lessons we can learn from people like doctors about alcohol? Give each of these statements a score for importance: 1, 5 or 10 by holding up fingers:
   - People can become addicted to alcohol.
   - Drinking small amounts of alcohol is safe for adults.
   - Drinking too much can damage your brain and body permanently.
   - Abusing alcohol can lead to accidents.
   - Some drinks are stronger than others.
   - Alcohol is expensive and it is illegal for young people to buy it.

Learning more

1) Name some drinks that have a low alcohol level (e.g. *beer, shandy, lager*); some which have a medium alcohol level (e.g. *wine, cider, Alco-pops*); and some with a high alcohol level (e.g. *spirits such as gin and vodka*).

NON-INTERACTIVE FOLLOW UP

Summary of the story

- Kasan went into town with his dad late on Friday night.
- The town was very busy with lots of young people on the streets.
- People were being rowdy, and were walking on the road.
- Many of the people had had too much to drink.
- Kasan saw a man nearly get knocked down by a car, and a girl being sick.
- Kasan's mum, a doctor, explained that alcohol is an addictive drug that affects the brain, and that too much can be dangerous and can damage the body.

Something to think about

1) What would you do if someone offered you lots of alcohol?
2) Why are the streets of our towns and cities so unpleasant on Friday nights?
3) How can young people be persuaded not to abuse alcohol?

Reflection

Look after your body and keep it safe – it has to last you a lifetime. Be aware of the dangers of alcohol and remember that, like many things, it is safe in small amounts.

Prayer

Lord God, please keep the teenagers and young adults of today safe from the risks of alcohol. Help them to be sensible about how much they drink. Help them not to become addicted. Please keep our streets safe at night. Amen.

3E TAKING RISKS

Objective
To help children recognise the risks in different situations.

PSHE/Citizenship links
3e (Risks in different situations)

Props
None

Introduction
We all take risks sometimes. Some risks are small and some are large. But which risks are worth taking? Today's story is about a group of extremely brave men who took a risk that probably saved the world.

TRUE STORY: THE HEROES OF TELEMARK

In 1943 the world was at war. Adolf Hitler's Nazi Germany had taken over several countries in Europe, including Poland, France and Holland, and had even tried to invade Britain. By this time, the USA had joined the war on Britain's side and the Germans were being pushed back. Hitler had only one hope if he was still to win the war against the Allies. He needed a special weapon, a weapon so terrible and destructive that no one would even dare to oppose his army: the atomic bomb. Both sides were locked in a desperate race to become the first to make the bomb.

Scientists in America were working on the problems day and night, and so were scientists in Germany. Both sides knew that special materials were needed and lots of equipment. One of the special materials is called 'heavy water' and Hitler had ordered a large amount of this to be made in a secret factory in a place called Telemark in Norway.

Norway was one of the countries that had been captured by the Nazis after fighting on Britain's side in the war. The Germans had taken over this mountainous country and had decided to use the power plant at Telemark as the place to make the heavy water they needed to build their first atomic bomb. It was a good choice: the factory was built high in the snow-covered Norwegian mountains, over a hundred miles from the nearest town. Very few people knew about it and it was almost impossible for the Allied soldiers to attack because of its remote position.

But the Allies – the British, Americans and Norwegians in particular, knew about the secret heavy water plant. Spies working in the factory sent information back to London at regular intervals. They knew that Hitler was trying to build an atomic bomb and they knew that he must be stopped at any cost. A plan was worked out. If the factory at Telemark in Norway could be destroyed, then the German scientists would not have the special heavy water that they needed and they would not be able to build the bomb.

There were many problems to overcome. The power plant was extremely difficult to find – even more so in winter when snow lay over everything in the mountains.

The Allied generals considered sending bombers to fly over the factory, but in those days aircraft did not have computers or special equipment to locate targets and also there was a chance that the freezing temperatures would ice up the planes.

It was decided that the best plan to destroy the factory lay with sending in small units of specially-trained soldiers with explosives to attack the target. But how could these soldiers get to the power plant without being seen? The factory was very heavily guarded by German troops and large guns. Would the soldiers even be able to find the remote factory in the mountains? It was clear that some very special people would be needed to carry out this daring raid – people who were not only brave, but who knew these mountains in Norway.

There were a number of Norwegians living in Britain at this time – these were people who had escaped the Nazis when Norway was invaded and had fled to the UK for safety. Among them were several soldiers who were outdoor survival experts. These men were quickly found and called to London to see if they were willing to accept the mission. The plan was explained to them: they would be dropped by parachute in the mountains in Norway, some distance from the power plant. They would then find a suitable landing place for two British aircraft full of commandos to land. Finally, they would guide these soldiers to the factory, attack it and destroy the heavy water machinery.

The five men agreed to accept the dangerous mission, even though they knew that the risks were enormous. After special training in Scotland, the men were flown to Norway and dropped by parachute into the mountains over 100 km from the power plant at Telemark. The men had huge packs to carry – they took tents, several days' food and weapons, as well as a large heavy radio to signal back to London to say when they were ready for the attack.

The winter of 1943 was particularly cold and the men had to march for miles in freezing conditions to reach a hut near the factory, where they could set up a base and search for a landing spot for the allied aircraft. Eventually the small group, led by Knut Haukelid, reached their destination. They found a place for the planes to land and signalled to London that the commandos could be flown over.

But disaster struck: there was a blizzard and one of the gliders carrying the British soldiers crashed, killing all of those on board. The other managed to land but the Germans were alerted by the crash and sent troops in who shot the remaining soldiers. The five Norwegians watched, helpless. Desperately discouraged, they returned back to their tiny mountain hut and radioed the bad news back to London. They were told to wait where they were until the bad weather improved and another landing could be attempted.

All through the terrible winter, the brave men struggled to survive. Their rations were long gone and they were weak from hunger. There were no plants to eat outside and the few animals that could survive in the snow were extremely difficult to catch. The men only survived by shooting a reindeer which passed near to the hut. They even had to eat the half-digested moss that was inside the reindeer's stomach.

In February, another group of specially trained Norwegian soldiers was flown into the area. After marching 50 km through snow and ice they joined up with the first small group, who had somehow survived for months in their hut. The attack was ready to go ahead. The soldiers had to reach the factory without being seen by the German guards and then climb the tremendously steep rocky hillside below the building at night, crossing a river to do so. Again, the risks were great, but the mission was vital.

With great skill, the Norwegian commandos reached the power plant and fixed explosives to the buildings. Timers were set, allowing them to escape, and the men scurried back down the mountainside under the cover of the trees. Several huge explosions ripped through the darkness – the mission was a success. The furious Nazis sent hundreds of troops and vehicles into the area to find the saboteurs, but the cunning Norwegians knew the mountains too well, and managed to hide before escaping back to Sweden and then Britain in small groups.

Hitler ordered the factory to be rebuilt but it was too late. The heroes of Telemark from Norway had held up the production of heavy water so much that the Germans were unable to build the bombs that would have killed millions and perhaps won the war for the cruel Nazis. A tiny group of brave men had saved the world.

INTERACTIVE FOLLOW UP ACTIVITIES

Questions

1) Why did the five Norwegian soldiers risk their lives?
   (Because only they had the knowledge to stop the Nazis building an atomic bomb.)
2) Did the men know how dangerous the mission was going to be?
   (Yes, they knew how hard it was to survive in the mountains and they knew the Germans were heavily guarding the plant.)
3) Why were these men chosen for the mission?
   (They were brave and they knew the mountains where the power plant was situated.)

Getting the message

1) What was the main message of this story?
   (That taking great risks is necessary if many people's lives are at stake.)
2) The heroes of Telemark took the risks they did because it was necessary to win the war and save the world. They were also experts who knew what they were doing. Sometimes we take unnecessary risks for no good reason at all. Which of the following risks is worth taking? Put up your hand for a yes and keep it down for a no.
   - Crossing a busy road between parked cars to save time.
   - Telling a lie to protect a friend.
   - Eating a hot curry.
   - Cycling in the dark with no lights.
   - Being cheeky to teenagers.
   - Taking one of your toys apart to fix it.

Learning more

1) Mini quiz: ask for 3 volunteers to come out and answer true or false to these questions about road safety risks:
   a) More road accidents happen during daylight than darkness. *(T)*
   b) 1 in 10 child pedestrian accidents happen on journeys to or from school.
      (False – it is 1 in 5.)
   c) Primary school children are good at estimating the speed of approaching cars. *(F)*
2) Crossing a busy road is a risky situation. Name some other risky situations.

NON-INTERACTIVE FOLLOW UP

Summary of the story

- Five Norwegians were flown to Norway during World War II for a secret mission.
- They were trying to stop Hitler's Nazis building the first atomic bomb.
- They destroyed a heavy water plant high in the mountains.
- They had to survive a freezing winter with very little food.
- Many people were killed during the operation.
- The mission was a success and the factory was partly destroyed with explosives.
- The men quite probably saved the world.

Something to think about

1) The heroes of Telemark took risks to save others. Do you take unnecessary risks?
2) Many children take dangerous risks when crossing the road.
3) If a situation is risky then find a safe place or get some help.

Reflection

Don't take risks that you don't need to take. Play safe by taking care of yourself, especially near traffic. You have everything to lose.

Prayer

Lord God, thank you for the brave heroes of Telemark who helped to win the war and save the world by risking their lives. Help us to keep safe and to avoid unnecessary risks, especially near roads. Amen.

3F PEER PRESSURE

Objective
To help children understand the dangers of peer pressure to behave in risky ways.

PSHE/Citizenship links
3f (Pressure to behave in unacceptable or risky ways)

Props
(Not essential): a cigarette packet

Introduction
Most adults who smoke cigarettes wish that they had never started. They find it very difficult to stop because cigarettes are addictive. Many of these people started smoking because it's what their friends were doing when they were at school. Some people took up smoking because they were put under pressure by other children just to look 'cool'. This still happens today. It's called 'peer pressure'. Some children from a primary school in London carried out a very interesting study on peer pressure as part of a big project called the Children's Parliament – here's what they found out:

A SCHOOL'S PROJECT ON PEER PRESSURE

We are from Miles Coverdale School and our contribution to the Children's Parliament is about 'Peer Pressure'. Peer pressure is a big problem if it means that children are doing something they don't really want to do.

We would like to begin by telling you the facts about peer pressure. We have researched these facts by watching plays, taking part in workshops, interviewing adults at the Urban Studies Centre and carrying out a questionnaire in our school. The research has taught us that peer pressure is a part of life. It happens to younger and older children than us, as well as adults. It will affect us at secondary school and its effect can be dangerous. We found out in our research that people get influenced to do things that they don't want to do – that is a negative type of peer pressure.

But peer pressure can also help – if there are children who can listen to you, who you can talk to and get help from, then peer pressure can be a positive thing. Through our School Council, Miles Coverdale School is looking at how peer pressure can help. It is called peer mediation – peer pressure that can make a difference.

To find out more about peer pressure we researched some of the problems young people face in their lives. The problems we researched included: Bullying, Stealing, Drug Abuse, Truancy and Racism.

We found that peer pressure can lead to all these problems. Our class visited the Urban Studies Centre where we interviewed five adults who know a lot about this subject:
- Bernie Baker, Hammersmith & Fulham Children's Rights Officer.
- Sara Hepburn, Hammersmith & Fulham Young Carer's Project Worker.
- Lily Makurah, Hammersmith & Fulham Tackling Teenage Pregnancy Co-ordinator.
- Gary McKenzie, Children's Society Campaigns Officer.
- Samm Postance, Police Officer and Borough Youth Officer.

We learnt that peer pressure is something that always seems to have been around. Many of the adults we interviewed had experienced a lot of peer pressure in their own lives.

When we interviewed two police officers about bullying, we learnt how often bullying happens and that it happens to young and old alike. Samm Postance, Community Police Officer, said:

"When bullies start bullying they don't stop to think what the victims feel like, they think more about what their friends are thinking."

At the Urban Studies Centre we asked Lily Makurah if she had been forced to do things she didn't want to do. She told us about how she bunked off secondary school with some friends and how she and her friends had bullied a new girl at primary school because the girl seemed different.

When we watched the play 'Wasted', the character Ryan started smoking cigarettes because he wanted to be part of a group. Later on we saw how hard it is to say 'no' when Ryan's friends were doing something. They all took drugs and he took them to be like his friends. Ryan ended up addicted to drugs. He had to steal money to pay for the drugs.

We carried out a questionnaire in school and asked our year 2, 3, 4, 5 and 6 classes about peer pressure. We asked each class what kind of things had they been made to do by their friends. We found that 33% had been dared to do something, that 23% had been made to steal by their friends, that 35% of the children had been rude to adults because of their friends and 15% had bunked off school with their friends. Makes you question who your real friends are.

We wanted to help children know more about peer pressure and the kind of problems they will encounter. We decided to design posters that explained these problems and showed some of the tactics you can use to help.

Each poster describes the problem and also has a 'helpful hand' to give the reader a few tips about how to cope with the problems. We are now using our computers to publish these posters on our school website.

Through the School Council, we are looking to train some children as mediators. These children will learn how to listen to other children's problems and help solve these problems by mediating with everyone concerned. This is another kind of peer pressure, what we are calling a positive kind of peer pressure.

So we would like to leave you with something we've learnt:
- Always try to be yourself.
- Always talk to someone about a problem.

[Edited extracts from http://www.la21.org.uk/cp2002/pressure.html]

INTERACTIVE FOLLOW UP ACTIVITIES

Questions
1) What is peer pressure?
   (When people of your age put pressure on you to do something.)
2) What kinds of problems does peer pressure cause?
   (Stealing, bullying, truanting, being rude, smoking, etc.)
3) Is peer pressure always bad?
   (No – peer pressure can be positive, e.g. friends talking to each other and helping with problems.)

Getting the message

1) What were the two important pieces of advice the children gave at the end of their project report?

   (1. Always try to be yourself; 2. Always talk to someone about a problem.)

2) Who can you talk to if you feel under pressure to do something risky? Give each of these people a thumbs up, a thumbs down or a flat palm (middle score) for how helpful they might be:
   - Close friend
   - Parent
   - The people who are putting you under pressure
   - An older brother or sister
   - A teacher
   - A group of school friends
   - Another adult you know, e.g. childminder, grandparent, or neighbour

Learning more

Some children are put under pressure to have the 'right' clothes or trainers. What effect does this kind of pressure have?

NON-INTERACTIVE FOLLOW UP

Summary of the assembly

- Some children from Miles Coverdale Primary School in London did a project on peer pressure.
- Peer pressure is a problem when it causes children to do something they don't really want to do.
- Peer pressure can lead children into bullying, smoking, drugs, truancy, stealing, and many other problems and risks.
- The children interviewed adults and carried out a questionnaire with children.
- They discovered that peer pressure is a widespread problem.
- Peer pressure can be positive, for example if friends listen to your problems and help you.
- Two ways to resist negative peer pressure are to be yourself – not someone always led by others, and to talk to other people if you do have a problem.

Something to think about

1) How can you help a friend who is suffering from peer pressure to do something dangerous?
2) Who is the best person to talk to if you have a problem with peer pressure?

Reflection

It is important to resist anyone who is trying to get you to do something you don't want to do. Always talk to someone at home or at school if you feel under pressure to take risks – don't let yourself be talked into trouble.

Prayer

Lord God, please help us to resist negative peer pressure and to provide positive peer pressure by helping each other. Help us to say no when we need to, so that we don't get involved in risky situations or break the rules. Amen.

3G SCHOOL RULES ABOUT HEALTH AND SAFETY

Objective
To help children understand the need for school rules about health and safety.

PSHE/Citizenship links
3g (School rules)

Props
(Not essential): yellow warning sign – 'Danger wet floor'

Introduction
Our school has special rules, which are designed to keep you safe. For example, we have a fire drill which we practice so that we can get out of the building quickly and safely if there is an emergency. We also have a rule that you mustn't run inside the building. Today's assembly starts with a special long poem called a cautionary verse about a boy who didn't obey this rule.

CAUTIONARY VERSE: RUSSELL WRIGHT, THE BOY WHO LOST HIS SMILE

This is the story of Russell Wright,
A boy with a cheesy grin,
Who didn't obey the rules at school
And dearly paid for his sin.

He was known as Rapid Russell
Since he never used to walk;
Running was the mode for him,
With the speed of a Champagne cork.

Outside on the field and playground,
Russell was simply a blur;
All you saw were his teeth flash past
And his legs in a mighty whirr.

Inside along the corridors
Of Russell's junior school,
He was virtually supersonic,
Which was strictly against the rule.

"Russell Wright, stop running!"
The staff would constantly squawk,
So he smiled his big wide cheesy grin
And tried to slow down to a walk.

"Russell we've told you a thousand times
Of the dangers of running indoors,
You're heading for an accident,"
Said the teacher from Class 4.

So Russell Wright would sheepishly stroll,
Until a corner or doorway appeared,
Then accelerate like a Ferrari,
While smirking from ear to ear.

"I'm the fastest kid in Bagley Heath,"
Was Russell's constant brag.
He also had the cheesiest grin,
Until he hit a snag.

It was a dull and showery April day,
With puddles outside by the score,
And moments after playtime,
Dark footprints speckled the floor.

The caretaker groaned when she saw them,
And went off to pick up her mop,
Along with the sign saying DANGER WET FLOOR,
While she prayed for the showers to stop.

Meanwhile, Russell the runner was restless
In the classroom just stuck in his chair;
He needed to stretch his jiggling legs
So he put his hand in the air.

"Miss, please can I go to the toilet?"
The teacher set down her white chalk
And repeated the mantra of Bagley Heath School:
"Very well Russell, but *walk!*"

Well, at least he walked out of the classroom
Before giving the corridor a grin;
Then Russell took off in his usual style,
Tearing along in a spin.

He saw the tall yellow caretaker's sign
Just as his feet left the ground;
And he wondered, just as his face hit the floor
If there was water around.

Russell Wright doesn't run any more,
Well, not at Bagley Heath;
And he certainly cannot give you a grin –
He hasn't got any teeth.

INTERACTIVE FOLLOW UP ACTIVITIES

Questions

1) What happened to Russell?

   (He slipped on the wet floor when running inside and broke his teeth.)

2) Did Russell know it was wrong to run indoors?

   (Yes, he was constantly being told by the teachers.)

3) What other accidents might Russell have had when running along school corridors?

   (Bumping into people; knocking over smaller children; running into people carrying hot drinks or fragile containers like glass bottles; spoiling displays; tripping; running into windows, etc.)

Getting the message

1) What can we learn from this poem?

2) Put your hand up if you agree with each of these statements about school rules:

   • School rules are to keep children safe.

   • School rules are to stop children having fun.

   • Practising fire drills is important.

   • Shouting in school is wrong because you might not be able to hear a teacher's instructions.

   • Teachers should decide all the school rules.

   • Children should have a say in deciding school rules.

Learning more

1) Why do children need to ask a teacher's permission to go somewhere like the toilet?

2) Are there any rules that are unnecessary?

NON-INTERACTIVE FOLLOW UP

Summary of the poem

• Russell Wright liked to run everywhere.

• The teachers told him to walk or he would have an accident.

• One wet day the corridor floor got dirty.

• The caretaker mopped the floor and left out a warning sign about the wet floor.

• Russell asked to go to the toilet and ran up the corridor.

• He slipped and smashed his teeth.

Something to think about

1) Why are school rules, like no running indoors, important?

2) What accidents can happen when people run indoors?

Reflection

The poem about Russell was funny but it had a serious point to make: school rules are there to keep us safe and to stop us hurting ourselves. Try to obey the rules so that you don't end up hurting yourself, or someone else.

Prayer

Lord God, help us to remember and to obey the school rules. Help us to resist the temptation to run and shout indoors. Thank you for taking care of us all. Amen.

4A How Actions Affect People

Objective
To help children understand that their actions affect themselves and others.

PSHE/Citizenship links
4a (How actions affect themselves and others)

Props
(Not essential): a bag of sweets and a chocolate bar or two and a small domino rally set up, maybe on a low table, so that it can be seen easily by all the children.

Introduction
Have you ever seen a 'domino rally'? It's where you knock a single domino over, like this *(demonstrate domino rally)*, and all the rest of the dominoes in the line get toppled over. One push affects every single domino. That's what it's often like with our actions. Listen to this story about how small actions can affect other people in big ways.

STORY: THE DOMINO RALLY

It was Saturday afternoon.

"Go on! No-one'll notice! It's only a couple of chocolate bars – what difference can it make? Anyway, it's always been alright before. Everyone does it! Just get a move on!" hissed Shona, as Jenny wavered at the sweetshop door.

"Ok, then, if you're sure," whispered Jenny, not sounding too convinced. She let herself into the little corner shop and sidled over to the stand where the chocolates were displayed. She put her bag onto the counter and rummaged around for her purse. "I'll have the usual Mars bar please, Jim," she said as she smiled sweetly at the boy behind the counter. "Oh, I'm sorry, I've only got a tenner. Could I have plenty of 5ps in the change, please? I need them for my bus fares," she added, when she gave him the money in exchange for the chocolate.

"OK," said Jim, "I've got plenty of change." He went round the corner to the till and picked out the correct money to give back to her. Those 5p coins were so fiddly! While he was busy counting out the change, and not watching her, Jenny quickly and skilfully grabbed several handfuls of whatever sweets were nearest and shoved them into her bag.

Her heart was thumping a bit when he turned to her with a handful of coins, but she flashed him her brightest smile and thanked him. "Bye then, see you in school on Monday," she said. "Hey I'm looking forward to your party next week – it's going to be a mega laugh!" she grinned, as she turned to leave the shop.

"Well, did you manage to get a good handful of chocs when he wasn't looking?" giggled Shona when Jenny appeared in the street again.

"Yeah," laughed Jenny. "They should keep us going all weekend – and more!"

And they did. The girls chomped their way through several chocolate bars as they sat and sniffed their way through the weepy video they'd rented. By the end of it they were feeling pretty sick, but they didn't let that stop them starting to plan the costumes they were going to wear at Jim's fancy dress party on the following weekend. They spent the rest of the evening in fits of giggles as they thought of more and more outrageously funny costume ideas. They had a fantastic night!

On Monday morning they were a bit surprised not to see Jim at school. He'd seemed OK when Jenny had been in the sweetshop on Saturday afternoon – perhaps he'd eaten something dodgy on Sunday, to make him poorly. Probably far too many chocolate bars from his dad's sweetshop where he worked at weekends… "Serve him right!" they giggled.

But he wasn't in school on Tuesday, Wednesday or Thursday either. "He must be really poorly!" said Jenny.

"I hope he's not so bad that his party's cancelled. I'm really looking forward to it and my costume's practically finished," said Shona. "He'd better be back by tomorrow!"

On Friday morning Jim did turn up at school, but he didn't look well at all. "Hey, Jim!" shouted Shona when they saw him. "You look dreadful, mate! Did you eat too many of your Dad's chocs and make yourself sick? I bet you just scoff them all the time, working behind that counter. That must be brilliant. You'd have to have eaten a fair bucketful to make yourself ill for that long, though!" she laughed.

"No, I haven't been ill at all," said Jim quietly.

"Oh, I see, just plain old skiving, then?" suggested Jenny.

"I wish!" sighed Jim. "No – it's a bit of a long story. We've been having a lot of trouble with the shop over the last few months. We've been losing loads of stock – probably kids coming in and nicking it. My dad's been getting more and more worried, because we're losing so much money. It's even affected his health – he's always at the doctor's because he's so stressed out. The stress has made him grumpier and grumpier at home, and there have been terrible arguments between him and my mum. She thinks he should get rid of the shop, because we're such a target for thieves, but my dad doesn't know what else he can do – he's not trained for any other sort of work.

"The last straw came on Saturday. We always do a bit of a stock-take on the last Saturday of the month and it showed that yet more stuff had been nicked: great handfuls of it. At first he gave me a really hard time and accused ME of having nicked it, or maybe given it to some of my friends."

"Oh that's AWFUL!" gasped Jenny, who was beginning to feel very uncomfortable.

"Yeah, it really upset me, because my dad has always trusted me before, but I'm sure he only said it because he was so upset. Anyway, I was denying having anything to do with it – and I guess I was shouting a bit, because I was upset too – when Mum came in and blew her top. She said she couldn't take any more of this stress, and that either the shop had to go, or she was leaving home. Poor Dad just didn't know what to say or do. Mum packed some clothes and walked out, to stay with a friend. She said that Dad has until the weekend to decide what he wants to do, because she can't live like this any more. That's why I haven't been at school – I just didn't think I could cope."

Jenny felt absolutely sick, and couldn't look Jim in the eyes. "Jim…" she muttered, "I… I just don't know what to say…"

"Aw, heck!" said Shona. "Your party's still going to be going ahead, though, isn't it?"

Interactive Follow Up Activities

Questions

1) Shona assured Jenny that it was OK to steal from the sweetshop. What reasons did she give? *(It's <u>only a couple</u> of chocolate bars – <u>what difference</u> can it make? Anyway, it's <u>always been alright before</u>. <u>Everyone does it!</u>).*

2) Shona asked "What difference can it make?" What difference did stealing the bars make? *(Jim was suspected by his dad – that hurt him, and it wasn't true; it added to Jim's dad's stress about the shop losing money; the stress was affecting the family, causing arguments etc; in the end it was one of the things that made Jim's mum walk out.)*

3) At the end, did either of the girls realise that their actions had had such a bad effect? *(Jenny realised that her actions had affected Jim's family very badly; Shona was still only interested in herself – the worst effect as far as she was concerned was that the party might be cancelled.)*

Getting the message

1) What was the main message of this story? *(Our actions affect both ourselves and others; sometimes actions that seem very small have a big effect.)*

2) Here are four messages: vote for the ones you agree with by putting up your hand:
   - You should try to think through anything you do before you do it.
   - It's OK to do whatever you want to whenever you want to.
   - Other people and their feelings matter: it's important to think about them.
   - It's a good idea only to do things that you'd be happy for someone else to do to you.
   - Just doing the odd little thing that's wrong doesn't matter to anyone – it's only big things that count.

3) Stealing affects other people; what other things can you think of that might affect others badly? *(E.g. lying, cheating, bullying, etc.)*

Learning more

How are the events in this story like the domino rally I showed you at the beginning? *(The theft of the chocolates was like the initial push on the first domino and all of the other things happened as a result).* Let's see if we can illustrate that: *ask children to name the events and ask each child who names one to come to the front:*
- Jenny stole the chocolates.
- Dad blamed Jim, probably because he was so stressed that the shop had been losing so much money for so long.
- Jim was hurt and shouted at his dad.
- Mum walked in on the argument.
- She couldn't take any more and left home.
- Dad has to decide if he wants to sell the shop and become unemployed or if he wants the family to split up.

Stand the children in a line, sideways to the audience, one behind the other. As you name each circumstance [e.g. a) Jenny stole the chocolates b) Dad blamed Jim], get child a to put their hands on the shoulders of child b. The next event is named (Jim was hurt & shouted…) and child b puts their hands on the shoulders of child c etc on to the end of the line, until all the children are linked. You can see how just pinching a few bars of chocolate is linked to all of these bad things.

NON-INTERACTIVE FOLLOW UP

Summary of the story

- Jenny stole chocolates from Jim's dad's shop, and she and Shona enjoyed eating them.
- Jim's dad blamed him for the missing chocolates at first.
- Jim's dad was very stressed because he was losing so much money at the shop.
- Jim's mum couldn't cope with the stress and told Dad to sell the shop.
- Jim's dad didn't know what to do: he was going to lose either that shop or his wife.
- Jenny felt guilty, but Shona didn't seem to care about Jim and his family.

Something to think about

1. Do you do small things you know aren't right, because you think they don't matter?
2. Think back over the last week: how many times have you done something that has affected someone else badly?
3. Jenny and Shona directly affected some people who they actually knew. Sometimes our actions affect people we will never even meet. Does that make a difference to how we should act?

Reflection

When you're tempted to do something that you think might not be good or kind, stop and ask yourself what effect your actions might have on other people. If you're not sure, ask yourself if you'd like someone to do that thing to you.

Prayer

Lord God, thank you for the people around us. Please help us to consider the feelings of other people and help us to act in ways that don't hurt them. Help us all only to do those things that we would like others to do to us. Amen.

4B People in Other Places

Objective
To help children think about the lives of people living in other places around the world.

PSHE/Citizenship links
4b (People in other places)

Props
None

Introduction
Most of you were probably born in this country and have lived here all your lives. Britain is a rich country compared to many others around the world, and the people who live here like you and me have a great deal of freedom. Adults in Britain are free to travel, and to earn and spend money; they can vote and have a say in how things are run in many ways. But what is it like to live in a very different country?

True Story: A Leaf in the Bitter Wind

Ting-Xing Ye was born in the big city of Shanghai in China in 1952. Her name means 'leaf' in Chinese. Her father owned a small factory and when she was a young child, her life was quite happy. But at this time in China there was something called a revolution. A group of men called communists took over the government of the country after lots of fighting.

The new government was led by a man called Mao. Mao's communist government said that people should not be allowed to own property and that everything should belong to the whole country. They took Ye's father's factory away from him. After this, Ye's life changed completely. The family now became poor. Ye's father was given a job in his own factory, but for pitifully low wages, and every day he was humiliated by the communists who had taken over the business it had taken him a lifetime to build up.

Ye's mother and father both became sick and the family could not afford a doctor or medicines. By the time Ye was 13 years old she was an orphan – both her parents had died. Ye was looked after by her great aunt.

Ye went to school in Shanghai and at first she did very well. But when Mao took over the country, the schools along with everything else changed. Mao wanted to show the world that China was a successful country and so he ordered everyone to join in with strange activities, which were supposed to prove that his communist ideas were right.

Here is one example: China has a huge population and feeding many millions of people took a great effort. Someone told Mao that birds were eating too many of the crops in the fields – sparrows in particular – and so Mao ordered everyone in China to kill sparrows. In Ye's school, lessons suddenly stopped and the children were ordered to kill sparrows. They were told to find nets and to make traps, and to throw stones and destroy nests. This may seem crazy to us, but it really happened. A lot of sparrows were killed, but it made virtually no difference to the amount of food that was produced.

Another year Mao became envious that countries like Britain and the USA were able to produce more iron and steel than China. He ordered everyone to help the country to make more iron. Once again, lessons in Ye's school stopped and this time a space was cleared in the playground to build a primitive furnace to make iron bars. No one really knew how to make iron but the school was still expected to do it.

Mao had soldiers and secret police everywhere who told the authorities if anyone, including children, were not working hard for Mao's Cultural Revolution, as it was called. So the furnace was built in the playground but there was nothing to put into it to make the iron bars. The local officials told people to bring anything made of iron or steel from home so that it could be melted down. People didn't want to do this, but the whole thing was like a competition and no one dared finish last or their names would be passed on to the soldiers.

Ye's house had already been searched and badly damaged by communist soldiers several times – they were looking for anything valuable that her father may have hidden. Furniture and precious pictures were destroyed. Ye's aunt was also told to take her cooking pots and her wok to be melted down for iron. At school, the railings were cut down too. The little school furnace, like many others, somehow managed to produce a few bars of useless, low quality iron. They were never used, but Mao was able to boast to the world that China was now a big steel-making country.

Ye and her three brothers were hungrier than ever, partly because there were no pans to cook with. And Ye was worried about her schoolwork. Making steel instead of doing lessons might sound like fun, but it was not. Ye desperately wanted to work hard to get qualifications and then find a good job – she knew it was her only hope of avoiding a life of endless drudgery and hunger.

But then things at school got worse. Grown-ups in China were expected to join Mao's Communist Party to show that they were loyal citizens. Everyone was given a little red book full of the sayings of Mao Tse-Tung or Chairman Mao, as he was known to the world. But many people didn't agree with Mao's ideas and a number of the teachers at Ye's school refused to join the party. Some of the older students who were communists began to spread rumours about these teachers, even writing them on the walls for everyone to see. The staff were too scared to complain and eventually most of these teachers disappeared, taken away by soldiers and never seen again.

So Ye's class was left without a teacher. She was fifteen years old. For days she turned up at school but there was no one to take the class. Her dreams of getting a good job were shattered. And worse was to come. Mao ordered that young people from the cities should be sent to the countryside to work on farms to grow more food. Ye was sent hundreds of miles away to a prison camp which had a farm attached to it. She had to work near the prisoners and was treated no better than they were.

The prison guards were cruel and Ye was forced to work long, back-breaking hours planting rice in wet fields. She was still only a child. Ye was trapped in this terrible place for years, never knowing what her future would be. So what happened to her?

Well, Ye's life was miserable but she did have a stroke of good fortune. One day, some books arrived at the prison camp. Ye was desperate to read something to relieve the boredom of her life. She found a book about learning English. Ye had always wanted to learn English. For years she studied this book, learning words and the way the language worked. It was extremely difficult as no one was there to help her.

But Ye did not give up and eventually she taught herself to read, write and speak English. She got hold of more books and she even passed an exam. At this time Chairman Mao wanted to become friendlier with the countries of the west, like America, and so he needed people who could translate Chinese into English. Very few people knew English in China at that time and Ye was offered a job at Beijing University to improve her language skills.

It was a dream come true for Ye. The bitter wind was still blowing little leaf, as she was known, but it did not blow quite so hard or so cold now.

Ye did well at University and even met English teachers from Europe and America. She then got a job working for the government, taking care of western visitors to China. She started earning money and she was able to see what rich and privileged lives the officials led while most people in the country went hungry.

Ye met a Canadian English teacher called William Bell and fell in love with him. He wanted to take her to live in Canada but China would not allow people to leave the country at that time, even though Mao was now dead. But William and Ye tricked the government. They made some documents, which said there was a grant of money for one person to study English in Canada for a year. Ye was allowed to apply for this work. She went to Canada but didn't return after a year. Instead, she settled down with William and now lives happily as a writer.

Her amazing story is written in an autobiography called *A Leaf in the Bitter Wind*. Make sure you read it when you're older.

INTERACTIVE FOLLOW UP ACTIVITIES

Questions

1) Why was Ye's life so hard when she was young?
   (She lost her parents; she was hungry; her schooling wasn't good; she had to work on a prison farm for years, etc.)

2) How was China different from Britain?
   (There was less freedom, the government controlled people's lives much more; there was less food & fewer possessions, etc.)

3) Who was Chairman Mao?
   (The leader of the Chinese Communist Party and the head of the country.)

Getting the message

1) Why was life so hard for many people in China like Ye?

2) There were many things that ordinary people were not allowed to do in Communist China in Ye's time. Put your hand up for the things which people were allowed to do: (✓ allowed):

   - Go to school ✓
   - Own a business like a factory
   - Read books ✓
   - Speak out against the government
   - Go to church
   - Travel where they wanted
   - Cook food ✓
   - Buy anything they wanted
   - Walk to work ✓

Learning more

1) Ye left China in 1987. Do you think that there are still any countries like Communist China in the world today?

(There are a few, e.g. North Korea.)

2) Married couples in China were only allowed to have one child in Ye's day. Why do you think this was?

(Overpopulation.)

NON-INTERACTIVE FOLLOW UP

Summary of the story

*   Ye Ting-Xing grew up in China in the 1950s.
*   She lost her parents when she was 13.
*   China was taken over by a brutal communist government led by Mao Tse-Tung.
*   Ye struggled at school because the teachers and students were always joining in with crazy government schemes.
*   Ye's class had no teachers at school and she was sent to a prison camp farm at 15.
*   She had to work hard and was treated badly; she was lonely too.
*   Ye learnt English from a book and got a place at Beijing University.
*   She worked for the Chinese government before escaping to Canada with an English teacher and becoming a writer.

Something to think about

1) What are the things we take for granted in this country?
2) How would you have managed in Ye's position?

Reflection

Ye Ting-Xing is a courageous woman who had to suffer a hard brutal life in communist China for many years. Remember that there are still many people in the world today who are treated cruelly and remember how fortunate you are to live in a country with so much freedom.

Prayer

Lord God, thank you for Ye Ting-Xing and her great courage. Thank you that we can learn about China through people like her who have told their stories. Please help those people around the world who are suffering today because of cruelty and injustice. Amen.

4B (2) PEOPLE IN OTHER TIMES

Objective
To enable children to understand what life was like for people in the past.

PSHE/Citizenship links
4b (People living in other times and places)

Props
(Not essential): an A-Z book or map, preferably of London

Introduction
Just imagine you're grown up, you've left school and you've just applied for a really good job. It's the job you've always wanted to do. You receive a letter asking you to come for an interview at the company's offices in London. The offices are in Zoffany Street. You've no idea where it is or how to get there. Well, most people would use a special map called a street atlas (*hold up the A-Z book/map*). Today's assembly tells the amazing true story of how the first London street atlas was made.

TRUE STORY: THE LONG JOURNEY FROM A TO Z

Phyllis was exhausted. Her feet were swollen and bruised. It was now nine o'clock at night and darkness had fallen on the streets of London. Phyllis put her notebook and pencil into her bag and headed home – she had been walking the streets for sixteen hours, starting at 5 in the morning, sketching the layout of roads, noting down names of avenues, squares, mews, cul-de-sacs and parks, as well as house numbers. Was it all worth it? Would her crazy plan work? Why was she doing this? The same questions went through her mind every night.

Phyllis Pearsall was born about 100 years ago. Her childhood was quite happy but, when she was 14, her father abandoned the family and moved to the USA. Her mother married another man who didn't like children. Phyllis was told that they couldn't afford the money to send her to school any longer and that she would have to find a job. Worst of all, her stepfather made it clear that he didn't want Phyllis around at home either.

Phyllis was clever, strong and independent, however, and since she was very good at languages, decided to move to France where she could get work teaching English to French students. At first she was lonely and badly treated, but she did manage to earn a little money. Phyllis also decided that what she really wanted to do was to become an artist.

When she was eighteen she moved to Paris, but she didn't know a soul in the great city and spent her first few nights sleeping on the streets under newspapers. Eventually, Phyllis found a room and began to paint and draw. Her work was good and she managed to sell a few pictures. She also wrote articles for newspapers and so was able to pay her bills and survive from day to day. Phyllis got married to another artist and they spent years travelling round Europe, painting and sketching the scenery. Sadly, the marriage didn't work out and in the mid 1930s, Phyllis decided to return to England.

There then came a very important day for Phyllis Pearsall. It was 1935 and Phyllis found herself trying to find a certain street in London. The ancient street map she had in her hand was useless – out of date – and Phyllis soon got lost. When she returned to her tiny bedsit flat she decided that what was needed was a proper up-to-date street atlas of London – and she was going to make it. It was a decision that would change her life.

Her friends and family said she was mad trying to make a map of London's streets all by herself, but Phyllis was determined. And so it was that she found herself walking miles and miles around one of the biggest cities in the world, drawing the pattern of roads, noting down names and features, listing everything carefully. It was an enormous task, and for a year, Phyllis mapped the capital, all 23,000 streets, often working for eighteen hours a day before returning to her little flat.

Of course, Phyllis had never made a map before and realised that she needed the help of an expert, so she approached James Duncan, a very good draughtsman who had once worked for her father. Mr Duncan was a funny man – quiet and stern, but he told Phyllis exactly what she needed to do, and he turned her sketches into proper drawings that would be suitable for printing.

One of the most difficult tasks of all was cataloguing all of the streets. For people to use the atlas easily, every road name would have to be put into alphabetical order to make an index. Phyllis spent hour after hour in her flat, writing the names onto cards and filing them in shoe boxes. One day, disaster struck – she was carrying a box of these cards over to Mr Duncan's house when she dropped it. All the 'Trs' went flying across the street. Luckily, Phyllis managed to retrieve them all, otherwise her London map might have been missing Trafalgar Square!

The whole task took over a year. Phyllis walked over 3000 miles altogether – that's like walking to America! There were more disasters to come too. At the printers, the wrong ink was used and the pages smudged. She couldn't afford a designer and so made the cover herself. She had also decided to call the book *The A-Z Street Atlas* and people, including her father, said this was a silly name. But worse was to come.

Phyllis paid for 10,000 copies of the book to be printed. With great excitement, she took a copy of it round the many bookshops of London. No one wanted to buy it. They said there was no call for a map like this. Some didn't take Phyllis seriously because she was a woman, working alone. She tried shop after shop without success. The books were piled high, all over her little flat – what was she going to do with them?

But Phyllis was never one to give up and someone suggested going to WH Smith's, the newsagents. "You'll have to see the buyer in his office," she was told. The buyer was a busy man and Phyllis spent whole days waiting in a queue to see him, never quite making it to the door. And then, it happened – somehow she found herself in the man's office, holding out her street atlas of London. He flicked through the pages carefully and looked up.

"We'll take 250 copies – sale or return." Phyllis was overjoyed. She delivered the books to the shop in a wheelbarrow – there was no money for a van. The books sold in a flash and Smiths ordered hundreds more, placing them in their stores around the city. Very soon, Phyllis's flat was empty – all 10,000 copies were sold – the atlas was a success!

Phyllis ordered some more to be printed, but she was exhausted with the strain of the work. She decided to employ a delivery boy and before long several people were working with her, producing the best-selling book. Phyllis formed the Geographer's A-Z Map Company, which is still going strong today.

World War II began soon after this, and all map production was stopped in case the enemy used the information in the atlas. After the war, there was another problem: a shortage of paper for printing. Phyllis discovered that she could get the atlases printed in Holland, however, and so the work continued. It was during a journey to Holland that tragedy struck Phyllis: the plane that she was travelling in crashed, leaving her in hospital with severe injuries: a fractured skull and spine.

After six months, Phyllis went back to work despite still being in constant pain. Sales were at least going well and the A-Z Company decided to make street atlases of other UK towns and cities like Birmingham, Manchester, Leeds and Glasgow. The money that Phyllis made from these atlases enabled her to continue her first love – painting, even though she still had terrible health problems from her injuries, including a period where she went blind for three months.

Life was never easy for Phyllis, even as a successful businesswoman and, as she grew old, she continued to work as hard as always, making sure that the shops never ran out of A-Z street maps. She also took great care of her workers and even left all her valuable company shares to the people she employed. Phyllis Pearsall died in 1996 – a truly remarkable person.

INTERACTIVE FOLLOW UP ACTIVITIES

Questions

1) Why do people still buy the A-Z street atlas of London today, nearly 70 years after it was first made?
   (It's such a large city; it's difficult to find your way around; there are many visitors; the map is easy to use and well designed.)

2) Why was it so remarkable that Phyllis's map succeeded?
   (She made it almost alone; it was very hard for a woman to succeed in business; people doubted her; she had no experience of map-making.)

3) What was it about Phyllis that kept her going, despite the many problems in her life?
   (Her character; hard work; determination; ambition; perseverance.)

Getting the message

1) What can we learn from this true story?
   (It's possible for one person to do something very difficult if he or she is determined; people can overcome problems in life; life was full of obstacles in the last century, e.g. the war, people's attitudes; don't give up!)

2) Show whether these statements about Phyllis are true or false by giving them a thumbs-up or thumbs-down:
   - Phyllis always wanted to make maps. *(F)*
   - Phyllis was given a lot of help by her parents. *(F)*
   - She didn't make any mistakes with her atlas. *(F)*
   - Phyllis proved a lot of London booksellers wrong. *(T)*
   - Running a business is easy. *(F)*

Learning more

1) Which of these three is the most important in being successful? *(Vote for each one, by putting hands up.)*
   - luck
   - hard work
   - knowing the right people
2) Why? *(Ask one person for each answer.)*

NON-INTERACTIVE FOLLOW UP

Summary of the story

- Phyllis was born in England in the early 1900s.
- Her father left home and Phyllis had to work in France when she was just 14.
- Phyllis became an artist in Paris and travelled round Europe.
- Phyllis got lost in London and decided to make a new street atlas.
- She drew maps and listed all 23,000 streets, walking round the whole city in a year.
- After being rejected many times, she sold thousands of copies of the book.
- She started the Geographer's A-Z Company, which is still going today.
- She overcame many difficulties, including the war, a serious plane crash and long illness.

Something to think about

1) What made Phyllis Pearsall a successful person?
2) Could you do the things that Phyllis did?
3) How do you react when you have difficulties?

Reflection

Phyllis Pearsall was a remarkable woman because she succeeded with a very difficult idea, despite huge problems. She overcame all the barriers through hard work, determination and belief in her own ability. Make sure you believe in yourself like Phyllis Pearsall did.

Prayer

Lord God, thank you for the wonderful inspiring example of Phyllis Pearsall's life. Please help us not to be put off achieving our dreams when obstacles get in our way. Help us to be hard-working, determined and strong. Amen.

4c FRIENDSHIP

Objective
To help children explore friendship and to develop skills to be effective in relationships.

PSHE/Citizenship links
4c (Types of relationship), 4a (Actions affect themselves and others)

Props
(Not essential): a friendship bracelet
(Needed for interactive follow-up): 2 placards saying **'GET LOST!' / 'CAN WE TALK?'** and a blank one.

Introduction
(Hold up friendship bracelet) Who knows what this is? What is it for? *(It's given by one friend to another, as a sign of friendship.)* It's wonderful to have friends. When things are going well, nothing's better than a good strong friendship. But what happens when you fall out? Listen to this poem by Allan Ahlberg:

POEM: SMALL QUARREL

She didn't call for me as she usually does.
I shared my crisps with someone else.

I sat with someone else in assembly.
She gave me a funny look coming out.

I put a pencil mark on her maths book.
She put a felt pen mark on mine.

She moved my ruler an inch.
I moved hers a centimetre.

I just touched her P.E. bag with my foot.
She put the smallest tip of her tongue out.

She dipped her paint brush in my yellow.
I washed mine in her paint water.

She did something too small to tell what it was.
I pretended to do something.

I walked home with her as usual.
She came to my house for tea.   *Allan Ahlberg*

Published in *Please Mrs Butler*, Allan Ahlberg (Kestrel, 1983), Copyright © Allan Ahlberg 1983.

Quick Questions:

1) How did this quarrel start?
   (She didn't call for her friend as normal.)
2) How did it continue?
   (Each girl reacted to her friend's actions by doing something else calculated to annoy.)
3) How can you tell it was only a 'small quarrel'?
   (Didn't escalate into real spitefulness; it 'blew itself out' and was resolved quite easily.)

It's not always that easy to get back on track again, though. Here's another poem by Allan Ahlberg about a friendship that's in a more serious mess:

POEM: IT IS A PUZZLE

My friend
Is not my friend any more.
She has secrets from me
And goes about with Tracey Hackett.

I would
Like to get her back,
Only do not want to say so.
So I pretend
To have secrets from her
And go about with Alice Banks.

But what bothers me is,
Maybe she is pretending
And would like *me* back,
Only does not want to say so.

In which case
Maybe it bothers her
That *I'm* pretending.

But if we are both pretending,
Then really we are friends
And do not know it.

On the other hand,
How can we be friends
And have secrets from each other
And go about with other people?

My friend
Is not my friend any more,
Unless she is pretending.
I cannot think what to do.
It is a puzzle.

Allan Ahlberg

Published in *Please Mrs Butler*, Allan Ahlberg (Kestrel, 1983), Copyright © Allan Ahlberg 1983.

Interactive Follow Up Activities

Questions

This poem focuses much more on what the girl feels about how things have gone wrong.

1) How does the girl feel about the break in the friendship?

(Sad, jealous, confused, etc.)

2) What could the girls do to start mending their friendship?

(Pluck up the courage to talk to each other, to see if they can work out what went wrong between them and what to do about it now.)

3) What might happen if neither of them dares to make the first move?

(It could be the end of the friendship.)

Getting the message

1) What was the main thought behind these poems?

(Friendships can go wrong; when they do go wrong, it can make us very miserable.)

2) Here are four statements about friendships: vote for the ones you agree with by putting up your hand:

- Friends are important to me.
- I never fall out with any of my friends.
- If I fall out with my friends, I sometimes feel like getting back at them.
- It's better to try to sort things out by talking than to give up on a friendship.

Learning more

1) *Ask for 3 volunteers to come out. Hand them each a placard, telling them not to show the words on them yet.* When you've argued with a friend, what's often the best thing to say to them? *Show placards one by one in order: a)* '**GET LOST!**' *b) the blank one (i.e. 'nothing') c)* '**CAN WE TALK?**'

2) I'm going to give you some ideas for making friendships work. Some of them are better than others! Give each of these ideas a score by showing fingers, as follows: I finger = a bad idea; 5 fingers = quite a good idea; 10 fingers = an excellent idea.

- Try to think how your friend is feeling, if you've fallen out.
- Talk about your friends behind their back.
- Be ready to say you're sorry if you've been a bit mean.
- Admit to yourself that you're not always perfect either.
- Tell your friends how important they are to you.
- Spread nasty rumours about your friends when you're annoyed with them.
- Remember that <u>all</u> friendships have their ups and downs.
- THINK HARD before you say something you might regret later.
- Try to treat people in exactly the same way as you'd like to be treated yourself.

NON-INTERACTIVE FOLLOW UP

Summary of the poems
- The first poem was about a small quarrel. It only lasted a day.
- The two girls spent all day doing little things to annoy each other.
- They were friends again by tea time.
- The second poem was about two friends who had stopped communicating.
- The writer of the poem is very miserable and wonders if her friend is miserable too.
- She doesn't know what's gone wrong, or what to do about it.

Something to think about
1) Had the two girls in the first poem ever actually stopped being friends?
2) When you've fallen out with someone, do you spend time thinking how *they* might be feeling?
3) Love your neighbour as yourself: what does that mean to you?

Reflection
Work on your friendships just as hard as you work on other things at school. Being a good friend is just as important as being able to read and do maths and science!

Prayer
Lord God, thank you for friends and friendship. Please help me to be a good friend: to be willing to talk and to listen, to admit my mistakes and to treat my friends in the same way that I'd like them to treat me. Amen.

4D BULLYING

Objective
To help children understand the nature and consequences of bullying.

PSHE/Citizenship links
4d (Bullying)

Props
None

Introduction
Some people think that bullying only involves physical things like pushing and hitting and fighting. But there is much more to it than that. Some of the worst bullying involves hurting people's feelings by things like name calling, accusing or making threats. Words can cause just as much pain as fists. The poem I'm going to read you was written by a girl who became a bully and didn't realise it – until she lost a friend.

POEM: ME, MY FRIEND & THE GIRL

I saw her as a threat to my
friendship with Jan
From the very first day she came
to our school
I didn't like her but Jan showed her around
"You're supposed to be my friend!"
I told Jan
"She's taking you away from me!"
But Jan just said I was being silly.
So, you see, I had to let the girl know
She wasn't wanted here, she was a friend thief
So I told her to get lost, to leave me
and Jan alone
She just started to cry like a baby.
I went on and played tricks on her
Kept telling her to go back to whatever
school
she came from.
Told her if she told the teachers I was
advising her to move
Then she would be a squealer.
She did
Once. And the teacher yelled at me.
Stupid teacher.
I went up to the girl.

"You're a squealer and a grasser."
I made sure everyone knew that.
I was happy because everyone agreed
with me.
Except Jan.
She didn't understand me; I didn't
understand her.
We didn't even speak to each other properly.
Even though we had been best friends before.
I blame the girl.
If she wasn't here, I'd still have
Jan as my friend.
Because you see, I still needed
Jan to be my friend.
But she stuck by the girl, took blame
for the girl.
And then she called me a bully.
Three years later, the girl and I are friends
now.
I never see Jan anymore, she'd moved.
When I look back, I see she was right.
I was a bully. But how did I become one?
Why didn't I stop? How did it end?
I still miss my friend Jan.

Adebayo Garuba

[Poem from http://www.bullying.newham.net/mempoems.htm]

This sort of thing happens all the time among friends – people get jealous and then start saying things that are wrong. They might make threats and regret it later. They might call people names because they are angry. But none of these things is right. Names and threats are ways of hurting people, and remember, some people are more sensitive than others. What might not hurt you, might cause tremendous pain to someone else.

INTERACTIVE FOLLOW UP ACTIVITIES

Questions

1) Why did Adebayo and Jan fall out?
   (Because Jan made friends with a new girl and Adebayo was jealous.)
2) What did Adebayo do to try to win Jan back?
   (Told the new girl to go away/get lost.)
3) What happened to Jan and the new girl?
   (Jan moved away; the new girl and Adebayo became friends eventually.)

Getting the message

1) Adebayo was called a bully by her own friend Jan. What could Adebayo have done differently at the time to stop this from happening?

2) For each of these statements, show a thumbs up if it is true and a thumbs down if it's false:
   - In the end Adebayo regretted being a bully. *(T)*
   - Jan was wrong to be friendly to the new girl. *(F)*
   - The new girl should have kept away from Adebayo and Jan. *(F)*
   - Jan probably wanted to be friends with both of the other two girls. *(T)*
   - Adebayo was right to call the new girl a friend thief. *(F)*
   - People need to share friends. *(T)*

Learning more

1) Is bullying when someone hurts someone else just once, or does it happen over a longer period? *(It is important to emphasise that 'one-off' incidents do not constitute bullying, but rather a series of actions, which hurt the same person, does.)*

2) If you do upset a friend or hurt someone, is there anything you can do to put it right?

NON-INTERACTIVE FOLLOW UP

Summary of the poem

- Jan and Adebayo were friends.
- A new girl arrived at the school and Jan became friends with her.
- Adebayo was jealous of the new girl's friendship with Jan.
- Adebayo was very unkind to the new girl – telling her to get lost, calling her names and playing tricks on her.
- The new girl cried and Jan looked after her.
- Jan stopped being Adebayo's friend and called her a bully.
- 3 years passed – Jan moved away and Adebayo and the new girl became friends.
- Adebayo missed Jan and she also realised that she had been a bully – something which she very much regretted.

Something to think about

1) How can you deal with jealousy?
2) What should you do if you see someone being bullied?

Reflection

Think about Adebayo. She lost a good friend, she was known as a bully and she deeply regretted hurting another girl. She wished she had never done it. Perhaps there is something unkind you have done recently which you will regret. You can undo the damage by saying sorry and being friends with that person. If you do this, everyone will feel much better.

Prayer

Lord God, thank you for the people around us. Help us not to hurt other people by saying things that are wrong. Help us to deal with jealousy and to share our friends. When we do hurt someone, help us to say sorry – give us the courage to own up and to make friends again. If we see someone else being bullied, help us to remember to tell a teacher. Amen.

4E CHALLENGING STEREOTYPES

Objective
To help children recognise and challenge stereotypical views of different groups of people.

PSHE/Citizenship links
4e (Recognising and challenging stereotypes)

Props
(Not essential): a book

Introduction
The word stereotype comes from printing. A printer would make a large printing block by putting together all the different letters that were needed and making a copy of them. The printing block would make copies which were exactly the same each time. These days, the word is used to describe how we look at people. A stereotype is someone we put in a category and think we know all about – but often we are wrong.

SIX STEREOTYPES

One stereotype is the troublesome teenage boy. Many people think that all teenage boys, especially those who hang around in gangs, are trouble.

- Jon is 16. He spent the last week of August in 2003 with a gang of his friends. But this was no ordinary gang – he was actually working with hundreds of other Christian teenagers to build a new skate park for children on a run-down housing estate in Salford. Jon enjoyed this so much that he has already decided to do this again in the future.

People often view people from other countries and places as stereotypes. One of the strongest stereotypes we have is that people from Africa are all poor and hungry. This is not true.

- Samantha Mumba is a pop singer who was born in Zambia, in Africa. She has been very successful: her first single went to number five in the UK charts and she has sold thousands of albums. She is clever, talented and certainly not poor!

Disabled people are often treated as stereotypes too. It is often thought that people who have physical disabilities – problems with their bodies – also have slow minds. Here is an example to show how mistaken this view is:

- Professor Stephen Hawking has motor neurone disease. He is confined to a wheelchair and can only speak with the help of a computer. But Stephen Hawking is a brilliant scientist, widely regarded as one of the cleverest people alive today.

Another stereotype concerns people with asthma. They are sometimes thought to be weak and unable to do sports. Again, this is not true.

- Paul Scholes plays football for Manchester United and England. He has scored over 100 goals and is rated by experts as one of the top midfielders in the world. Paul has asthma and has to use an inhaler, but this hasn't stopped him playing the game he loves.

Girls and women sometimes suffer from a stereotyped view. Especially in the past, many people believed that women were not brave or strong enough to do tough jobs carried out by men.

- Ellen MacArthur is now a famous woman. In the year 2000, she sailed right round the world alone in a yacht. She made this remarkable journey in 94 days, which was 11 days faster than the previous record. Ellen had to face many great risks such as enormous ocean waves, fierce storms and dangerous rocks.

A lot of children think that elderly people are slow and lead dull lives.

- Frank Benson is 74 years old. He plays table tennis in the Ryedale League in Yorkshire and his team have been champions for five years in succession, with Frank winning over 80% of his games, mainly against much younger players. Frank is retired but he is always busy: he makes wooden furniture and writes a column in the local newspaper.

INTERACTIVE FOLLOW UP ACTIVITIES

Questions
1) Who can remember the name of one of the people you've just heard about?
   (Jon, Samantha Mumba, Stephen Hawking, Paul Scholes, Ellen MacArthur, Frank Benson.)
2) What are stereotypes?
   (When we think of people as being of a certain type and we prejudge them; people put in narrow, simplified categories which are generally not fair or true.)
3) Why should we avoid stereotypes?
   (It is wrong to judge people without knowing them; they can give people a bad name; they can prevent people from getting opportunities in life, e.g. good jobs.)

Getting the message
1) What can we learn from these six people's lives?
   (That stereotypes are not real people; that people are all different; that using stereotypes is unfair.)
2) Show whether these statements about people are stereotypes by putting your hand up:
   - Homeless people are often seen as lazy and dirty. *(T)*
   - Irish people are often seen as clever and fashionable. *(F)*
   - Rich people are often seen as posh and greedy. *(T)*
   - Asian people are often seen as British and good English speakers. *(F)*
   - Short people are often seen as young and cute. *(T)*

Learning more

1) Where do you often see or hear stereotypes?
2) How can you avoid stereotypes?

NON-INTERACTIVE FOLLOW UP

Summary of the assembly

- A stereotype is a narrow, simplified view of a type of person.
- The stereotype of a teenage boy in a gang is a troublemaker – Jon proved that they are not all like this.
- The stereotypical African is poor, uneducated and hungry; Samantha Mumba the pop star is none of these things.
- Disabled people are often stereotyped as being less capable than others – Professor Stephen Hawking shows this view to be false.
- People with conditions like asthma are sometimes stereotyped as being weak and unable to play sport – Paul Scholes doesn't fit this picture at all.
- Girls and women suffer from the stereotype of not being brave and strong – Ellen MacArthur is both of these.
- Elderly people are sometimes thought of as boring and slow – not Frank Benson.

Something to think about

1) Why should we avoid stereotypes?
2) Do you think of some people as stereotypes?
3) Do people stereotype you and how can you prove them wrong?

Reflection

Learn from these six remarkable individuals that thinking of people as stereotypes is unfair. Think of people as unique individuals – each one different, each one with their own qualities and abilities. Value everybody.

Prayer

Lord God, thank you that you have made each one of us so different. Please help us to avoid stereotypes, but instead to treat people as individuals, each one different and special. Help us to value all people, including people from other cultures, people of other ages and people with other interests. Amen.

4f Differences Between People

Objective
To help children learn that the differences and similarities between people arise from a number of factors, including cultural, ethnic, racial and religious diversity.

PSHE/Citizenship links
4f (Differences and similarities between people)

Props
None

Introduction
There is an amazing variety of different people in the world. In the UK we can meet people from all over the planet – from every continent – because it is now so easy for people to travel. But often we know very little about the background of the people we see around us. Let's discover the story of one very interesting person who now lives in the UK.

True story: Shaheen Ali

Shaheen Ali is a mother. She has three children who are now grown up and finding their own way in life. Shaheen was just four years old when she became engaged to be married to her cousin Sardar. It was her grandfather's idea that she should marry Sardar when she grew up. The couple did eventually become husband and wife when Shaheen was 19 years old. This type of marriage was a normal custom in that time in the country where Shaheen was born.

Shaheen Ali has dark hair and light brown skin. She was born in Pakistan, in the mountainous North West Frontier Province. All of Shaheen's family have a similar complexion and the same dark hair, as does almost everyone else from that region. Just as most people from central Africa have dark skin and many people from Scandinavia have fair hair, it is just another example of the huge variety in appearances of different people around the world.

Shaheen Ali is now a professor. She is Professor of Law at Warwick University in England. Shaheen was sent to a good school in Pakistan where she grew up and she worked extremely hard, passing all of her exams with very high marks. The school was run by Catholic nuns who taught Shaheen a great deal about other countries, particularly about the culture of Europe. When she left school, Shaheen went to study Law at Peshawar University in Pakistan. After this she wanted to find a job in Europe, where she would have a chance to find out about international law – laws all over the world. Warwick University realised what an exceptional person she was and gave her a job in this country.

Shaheen Ali is a Muslim. Pakistan, where she grew up, is a Muslim country where most people follow the religion of Islam, and Shaheen and her family now follow their faith in Britain. Shaheen wears the brightly coloured clothes, including saris, which nearly all women from her region of Pakistan wear. She sometimes covers her head with a veil when she returns to Pakistan, which is another Muslim tradition of that country.

Shaheen Ali speaks four languages. There are many languages in Pakistan and when Shaheen Ali became a government minister there for a number of years, knowing the different languages spoken in the various regions of the country was very helpful to her, especially when she wanted to hear the concerns of ordinary people. Shaheen is fluent in Urdu, Pashtu, Punjabi and English. She can read and write Arabic and has a working knowledge of Persian too. Shaheen's English is particularly good and, like nearly all people from Asia, she speaks it with a slight accent, just like most people from the UK speak French with an English accent.

There are many other remarkable things about Professor Shaheen Ali: she was the first female professor of law in Pakistan, the first female government minister in the North West Frontier Province and first female Pakistani to become a professor of law in the UK. She is also an international expert in gender equality and human rights and frequently travels around the world giving lectures.

Professor Ali is also, as we've learned, a mother and married as well. So she's a very special person – unique, just like every other person on the planet – but now you know a little bit about how she came to be the person she is.

[Inspired by a Warwick Graduate Association magazine article by Chris Arnot, October 2003.]

INTERACTIVE FOLLOW UP ACTIVITIES

Questions
1) Why does Shaheen Ali wear a sari?
   (It is a traditional dress of Pakistani Muslim women.)
2) How did she get to be a professor?
   (She worked very hard at school and went to university and she also worked as a government minister and at other universities.)
3) Why is Shaheen Ali regarded as a remarkable woman?
   (Because she has held so many important jobs and was the first Pakistani woman to become a professor of law in the UK.)

Getting the message
1) Why is Shaheen Ali different from many other women in the UK?
2) Put your hand up when you hear a true statement:
   * Shaheen Ali was brought up in Britain. *(F)*
   * More than one language is spoken in Pakistan. *(T)*
   * Working in different countries has helped Professor Ali to understand international law. *(T)*
   * All Asian women are Muslims and wear saris. *(F)*
   * Pakistan and Britain have different cultures. *(T)*

Learning more
1) Do British people go to Pakistan to work? *(Yes)*
2) Why do people sometimes not understand people from another culture or race?

112

NON-INTERACTIVE FOLLOW UP

Summary of the story
- Shaheen Ali is Professor of Law at Warwick University in England.
- She was brought up and educated in Pakistan.
- Shaheen Ali is a Muslim, like most Pakistani people.
- She is married and has three children.
- Shaheen speaks four languages and is a world expert on international law.
- She was the first female Pakistani to become a law professor in the UK.
- Professor Ali was also a local government minister in her country.

Something to think about
1) Why is knowing a person's background often helpful?
2) Why is Shaheen Ali unusual?

Reflection
Knowing Shaheen Ali's background is very interesting and also helps us to understand what kind of person she is. She is an amazing person who has achieved such a lot in her life, but you cannot tell this just by looking at her. Remember the saying: do not judge a book by its cover.

Prayer
Lord God, help us to learn about the background of different people, and help us to understand and respect different cultures. Help us also not to judge a person just by looking. Amen.

4G GETTING HELP AND SUPPORT

Objective
To help children learn where they can find help and support.

PSHE/Citizenship links
4g (Where individuals, families and friends can get help and support), 4f (Disability)

Props
(Not essential): Jacqueline Wilson's book *The Worry Website*

Introduction
Everybody has worries from time to time. It is quite normal to worry about all sorts of things: friends, family, what you look like and growing up, for example. Lots of children also worry about school, and today's assembly features part of a story about a girl who has a worry connected with school. It's from a book called *The Worry Website* by Jacqueline Wilson. The book features a teacher called Mr Speed who sets up a website for the children in his class to send in their worries…

EXCERPT FROM THE WORRY WEBSITE: NATASHA'S WORRY

Type in your worry:
I wish I could take part in the concert.

Mr Speed is organizing a concert. The whole class keeps going on about it. William is fussing because he can't do anything. Everyone else is singing or playing a musical instrument or reciting a poem or dancing. I can't sing or play or recite or dance. But people don't expect me to be able to perform. I can't even walk or talk. But it's OK. I manage. I use a wheelchair. It's electric and powerful so sometimes I can muck about chasing the other kids. I have a special speaking machine too. My fingers work in a shaky sort of way so I can press the right button and words get said. Not always the words I want. I can't say rude words when I'm cross unless I spell them out laboriously. I usually choose to say short easy words because it's so much quicker.

It makes me sound a bit simple. I know I look it. But I'm NOT. I go to a special school but we have proper lessons, Maths and English and Science and stuff just like everyone else. And one day a week I go up the road and round the corner to Mapleton Juniors to see what it's like in an ordinary classroom.

Only it's not the slightest bit ordinary. They have this really wacky teacher Mr Speed. I wasn't sure I liked him at first. He leaps about a lot and shouts and uses weird long words. The teachers and helpers at my special school walk carefully and talk quietly and use words everyone can understand. I got a bit nervous when he came near me at first. My arms jerked about more than usual and I shrank down even more than usual. Most people think I'm younger than I am because I'm quite little. They treat you like a baby anyway if you use a wheelchair.

But not Mr Speed.

"Hello Natasha," he said, straight to me. Lots of people look at Wendy, my helper, even though they're talking to me.

I made my machine say hello back. Mr Speed told the class about my talking machine and asked if I'd say hello to them too. I did. Then I added, "Let's make friends." This was artful. I knew they'd all go, "Aaah!" and say yes. You need to get children on your side. Sometimes they can be sooo mean. They call you Spaz and Dummy and The Veggie. You can't have thin skin if you have a disability. Sometimes I've had to have skin like a *rhinoceros* to stop all the rude remarks hurting me.

But Mr Speed's class were all good to me right from the start. Almost too nice. The girls begged Wendy to let them push me around and they treated me like a doll, fussing with my hair and fiddling with my chair strap and speaking very loud and very s-l-o-w-l-y. The boys waved at me a bit nervously, keeping well clear of my wheel chair – in case I leapt up and bit them? They were all ever so polite though – apart from William. He didn't mean to be rude. He isn't that sort of kid. He just stared and stared and stared at me, as if I was an extraordinary television programme. The pretty girl, Samantha, gave him a little nudge and whispered to him not to stare so.

"Why?" said William.

"Because it's rude," Samantha hissed.

"But she looks so *funny*," said William.

"Sh!" said Samantha, going pink.

"She can't hear, can she?" said William. "She can't *speak*."

[Excerpt from *The Worry Website* by Jacqueline Wilson, pp.106-109, Corgi 2003. Reproduced by permission of David Higham Associates.]

Of course, that isn't the end of the story about Natasha and her worry. She finds a special friend and together they talk about their troubles. If you want to find out what happens and if Natasha gets to be in the concert, you'll have to read the story – remember, the book is called *The Worry Website* by Jacqueline Wilson.

INTERACTIVE FOLLOW UP ACTIVITIES

Questions

1) Why is Natasha worried about being in the concert at school?
   (Because she is disabled and thinks she probably won't be able to take part or won't get a chance.)

2) How do the children in Mr Speed's class treat her?
   (They treat her well, but fuss over her and speak to her as if she's much younger; the boys are polite but wary.)

3) Why does Natasha say that she needs thick skin like a rhino sometimes?
   (Because some people call her rude names and having a thick skin means you don't let this behaviour really hurt or upset you.)

Getting the message

1) Natasha is worried about being in the concert – who should she talk to about her worries? *(Her friends, her family, her teachers, the people running the concert, Wendy, as many poeople as possible who might be able to help.)*

2) How can you deal with worries? Give each of these ideas a thumbs-up, a thumbs-down or an 'in-the-middle' (flat hand).

   - Just try to forget them.
   - Tell your best friend what your worries are.
   - Ignore the situation and hope it will sort itself out.
   - Talk to someone at home in a quiet moment.
   - Go to a worry website or telephone advice service.
   - Tell anyone who will listen.

Learning more

1) If Natasha told you her worries, what would you say to her?

2) The class weren't sure how to treat Natasha because she was disabled. How can you find out how a disabled person would like to be treated?

NON-INTERACTIVE FOLLOW UP

Summary of the story

- Natasha went to the Worry Website because she was worried about being in the school concert.
- Natasha is disabled – she can't walk and so has a wheelchair, and she needs a machine to help her talk.
- She goes to a special school and has an adult helper called Wendy.
- Mr Speed the teacher made Natasha nervous at first, but she likes him now.
- The girls and boys in Mr Speed's class were nice to her but weren't sure how to treat her.
- A boy called William was rude to her because he thought she couldn't hear.

Something to think about

1) Who's the best person to talk to if you have worries?

2) Where can you get help if there's something at school you're worried about?

Reflection

Try not to keep worries to yourself – you'll feel better for sharing them and the people you talk to might be able to help you. Tell someone you trust about your worries, however silly you think they are, and be prepared to listen to other people's worries too.

Prayer

Lord God, please give help and courage to everyone who has worries. Help us to share our worries and to listen to other people who want to share their problems with us. Lead us to find answers and to help each other with all our worries. Amen.

Badger Publishing Limited
26 Wedgwood Way, Pin Green Industrial Estate,
Stevenage, Hertfordshire SG1 4QF
Telephone: 01438 356907
Fax: 01438 747015
www.badger-publishing.co.uk
enquiries@badger-publishing.co.uk

Badger Assembly Stories with Citizenship and PSHE themes
Ages 7-11
ISBN 1 84424 240 4

Publisher: David Jamieson
Editor: Paul Martin
Designer: Adam Wilmott

Printed in the UK.

For details of the full range of books and resources from

Badger Publishing

including
- Book Boxes for Infants, Juniors and Special Needs
- Badger Nursery Rhymes - A3 cards and teacher book
- Full Flight for reluctant readers
- Badger Religious Education – course for the primary school
- Teaching Writing - ten books for Y1 - Y6
- Writing Poetry – four books for juniors
- Badger Fiction for KS2 - new fiction and teacher books
- Delbert's Weekly Worksheets for the Numeracy Hour and Practice Questions for KS1 and KS2 Maths SATs
- Badger Maths: Problem Solving Book 1 and 2
- Badger Key Stage 2 Revision Quizzes for English, Maths and Science
- Badger ICT - colourful course for Y1 - Y6
- KS2 Test Revision Guides - Writing and Maths: Using and Applying Basic Background Knowledge - History, Geography
- Badger Assembly Stories - for KS1-2

See our full colour Catalogue available on request

Visit our website
www.badger-publishing.co.uk

Badger Publishing Limited
26 Wedgwood Way, Pin Green Industrial Estate, Stevenage,
Hertfordshire SG1 4QF

Telephone: 01438 356907   Fax: 01438 747015

enquiries@badger-publishing.co.uk